WALKING WITH ROCKS

An English Woman Loose in the Woods

Esther Parry

'

HANNAH AND REBEKAH

Thank you for encouraging your crazy mother to go on this madcap adventure. Your support carried me over every single rock in my path…including the ones in my head. You're just the best!

Contents

"But those who hope in the Lord
will renew their strength.
They will soar on wings like eagles;
they will run and not grow weary,
they will walk and not be faint."

Isaiah 40:31
The Bible New International Version (NIV)

INTRODUCTION

Right, I'm going. That's it. Finally, decision made.

Most people have a sensible mid-life crisis, like buying a fast car or a round the world luxury cruise or something. Not me. Next year I'll be fifty and I want to do something slightly crazy to mark half a century on the planet. I'm planning a bit of a walk, a little trundle in the woods…the wild woods…in America…with bears, and ticks, and rattlesnakes. And if you're reading this, I probably made it out alive and hopefully got to the end. I'm planning on "Thru-hiking" the Appalachian Trail, that's 2192 miles…in one year. And why would any sane human being want to do that? Good question, exactly why *am* I doing this??? I guess you need to know a little bit about me first to answer that.

So, here I sit, a middle-aged woman, at the end of some things, still in the middle of a few, and at the beginning…of what? Five years ago, if anyone had predicted my life right now, I would have questioned whether they understood how reality works, and whether they knew me as a person at all. My marriage was down the pan and beyond redemption. It'd been that way for years. Meagre self-esteem and a profusion of self-doubt had me stuck there, like chewing gum in hair – pulling this way and that, trying to find a means of extraction without chopping off another chunk of the diminishing remainder of me. Then, a chance conversation and suddenly I find myself applying for an undergraduate degree. Through each step of the process I expect the door to slam firmly shut on what seems, to me at least, to be an over-ambitious enterprise. An enterprise that's got its roots firmly anchored in a completely different universe to the one that my comfort zone is currently living in. But the doors don't slam. I get an unconditional offer to study Biological Anthropology at the University of Kent, England. I take it. Along the way, I learn that I'm a lot more tenacious than I thought I was, and a lot brighter than I'd hoped to believe, and three years later I pass with first class honours. Outside Uni, I become part of an amazing group of friends. They're kind, funny and challenging, and they remind me that it's good to be me. I finally find the courage to end my marriage. Slowly I become comfortable in my own skin once again, and I remember that people don't always have an agenda, that sometimes they're just nice, because they don't have, and don't need, a reason to be anything else.

I get a job working part time at a wildlife conservation park and fall in love with a couple of big brown bears. They inspire me. They come from a life of horrendous deprivation and yet they recover, they adapt, and they thrive. I admire their ability to leave behind what's passed and embrace each moment they're living in now with vigour and hope. I discover that I love to talk to strangers, that even in a brief moment a connection can be made between human beings. With a smile. With a story. I persuade petrified children and their nervous grownups, who are unconvincingly feigning bravery, to drop off the ledge of a stomach churningly high vertical drop slide. I watch their faces as they gain a ton of confidence and return to the top smiling and feeling invincible. I remember that I love to encourage people to see their own potential, their worth and their value, and to see them learn that they are so much more than who they thought they were. The rest of the time I'm delivering shopping for one of the big supermarket chains. There's never enough time, the vans are elderly, the traffic's horrendous, there's heavy lifting, and the pay wouldn't keep a dormouse alive. But I love it. I see a six-minute snapshot of people's lives; they say more than you would imagine in that tiny window. They say more than they think they do too. All with a story. All with their own particular brand of reality. Safely interacting with the stranger standing in their doorway, knowing that they'll never come across me in 'normal life'. Even the ones that say nothing have a hint of their story etched on the expressions they wear, in the lines drawn out on their faces. For someone like me, with a creative mind and a healthy imagination, they are gold. Each person a treasure trove of human experience. Waiting for affirmation, a listening ear, to dump, to vent, or just irritated because I interrupted their favourite TV programme. And my colleagues? Quality people, all with their own stories too, just as I have mine. Maybe it's the anthropologist within me? What's not to love?

I remember when I was really young, I wanted to be an explorer. I wanted to go to the Amazon jungle. That was my dream, my ambition, to discover hidden places no one else had ever seen or heard of. It excited me, the possibility of daring to face down monsters lurking in the rivers and trees, immersed in a world without a human signature, a raw, honest, bare place, where your mettle was tested and there were no prisoners. I guess that wasn't exactly the way I described it at the tender age of five or six, but it's what I would have written if I could have articulated my dreams. As I grew, my ambitions changed but the theme of exploration ran through them nevertheless; palaeontologist, marine biologist, the Air Force, a life off the grid in Tibet - not your stereotypical aspirations for a woman.

In my first year at secondary school, when I was about twelve, I remember a project on Amazonian Indians. They lived off the land and shrank the heads of their unfortunate enemies. I worked so hard on that assignment. It was the inspiration behind the choice of my degree subject. I kept the exercise book for years and only threw it out after I got my BSc. I wanted to be able to live like that, resourceful and self-sufficient. Threads of that desire subliminally wove their way through my life. For many years I produced and processed all the fruit and veg I needed. I grew tiny plants from seed, potting and re-potting until my conservatory resembled its own kind of jungle for a couple of months of the year. I'd make things from scratch wherever I could – beer from nettles, toys from wood and wool, I even built a couple of computers from bits. Always thinking outside the box; if I didn't have it, I'd think of a way I could make it. As a single parent my financial resources were seriously limited and this often pushed me to devise 'off the wall' work arounds. That gift probably came from my dad who was pretty good at making things happen with the ingredients he had to hand, figuring things out for himself, doing it his way. I tell you, if he fixed it even the cockroaches that people say would survive a nuclear holocaust would die before it fell apart! There's a crazy paving patio and a cast concrete block wall in the front garden of a house in Epsom, Surrey, that he built around the time I was learning to ride my first mini tricycle; it's still there to this day.

So, there you go, the wanderlust within me has always been there. It's ingrained in my soul, apparently, as is the hunger for the liberty of a life that relies less on stuff and more on wits. I like to think of it as a connection with my distant relatives who lived in caves all those millennia ago; moving from place to place following their food around, hunting mammoths, and leaving enigmatic records of their exploits on rock walls because kindle hadn't been invented yet.

Anyway, back to the original question – why am I going

to walk the Appalachian trail? I guess I've answered it on a superficial level - I'm satisfying the drive inside me that's never been happy with the mundane, with the party line, with cultural conformity. But really, that's not it.

The whole thing was just a thought, a pipe dream really, that came up in a conversation during a small midweek church homegroup meeting one evening two, maybe three years ago now. I can't even remember what we were talking about at the time, but I do remember saying that I wanted to test my mettle and discover who I am, truly am. I wanted to know if I could cut it if it was just me, God and nothing else. For thirty-five years, since I decided, at fifteen, that I was going to put God in charge of my life, my faith has carried me through the great, the terrible, and the mundane days of my life. Not that I'm your stereotypical 'Christian' though; I guess I might have caused the odd raised eyebrow once or twice with my interpretation of what that word looks like lived out. I don't talk much about my faith unless people ask or it comes up in the natural course of a conversation, but that belies the true depth of its importance to me. I don't exaggerate when I say that it's what has saved me from a life at the bottom of a bottle of pills, or worse, from becoming the reason for a train driver's PTSD. I feel and think deeply, I reckon I make the Mariana Trench look like a shallow muddy puddle, and that makes it hard for me to live with me. I still struggle, but those struggles make me who I am, and I'm learning that when I'm walking in a storm, I don't have to let that storm into the inside of me, but I do have to ride it out. That's something I can't do by myself and my faith means I never have to.

So, I know who I am, but I need to *know* who I am.

That's why I'm doing this.

That, and because it's about the most epic and exciting thing I've ever even contemplated. I'm going to have to die at some point I guess, and I'd rather go out doing something interesting like falling off a cliff with spectacular views on the way down, or maybe having my torso scythed to bits by a bear's five-inch claws and two-inch teeth than in front of the TV watching Bear Grylls. Did I mention my healthy imagination?

CHAPTER ONE

Surely you just need a pair of walking boots, right?

When one decides to undertake a bit of an adventure the whole process seems to go through a series of phases. Initially you're all gung-ho and excited. You're going to do this, what could possibly go wrong? How hard could it be? In my head I've already grabbed an oversized bandana, emptied the contents of my larder into it, tied up the four corners and slipped it onto a long pole that I've got hoisted over my shoulder. I've put on my muddy walking boots …because of course I'm an avid walker managing four miles two or three times a week up the local woods, and this uniquely qualifies me to walk the length of an entire mountain range…and all I need now is a plane ticket. WRONG. Very, very wrong.

Slowly, it dawns on me that watching Bill Bryson's "A Walk in the Woods" does not qualify as adequate research, and Googling 'How to walk the Appalachian Trail' turns up a mountain (ha-ha...) of overwhelming information. Questions that weren't even on my radar pop up on the screen and I begin to realise that this is not, in fact, the advertised "walk in the woods" that I thought it would be.

I guess the information I had at the beginning was that the Appalachian Trail is a very well signposted and very well-maintained long-distance trail in America. Although this *is* to all intents and purposes true, there's a lot that no-one seems to mention…a series of elephants in the room I am to discover, looming large and obstinate in my path along the way. I ask myself many times in the next few months whether people just forget this stuff when they get home or whether I'm the only one that's a bit naïve when it comes to my expectations.

During my research, the first thing that I notice is the absolute obsession with weight. Not your own body's weight, oh no, it's the sum total weight of the man-made hermit crab shell of a container and its contents that I'm going to become very well acquainted with for the next half a year. There are pages and pages of advice, information, suggestions, all basically persuading you that if you don't cut out the labels from your clothes to save those two extra grams you have only yourself to blame when your knees buckle and your ankles give out.

There are those who pack 'lite', and *then* there are those who pack 'ultra-lite'. Backpacks thinner than clingfilm and tarp-tents that a homeless person would find unacceptable to live in. Stoves the size of a packet of cigarettes…and even that is deemed a luxury by some who choose to re-hydrate their food in cold water. Yuk. Cold mashed potato? Cold oatmeal? Really?? Are they serious??? And the more one pays the less one gets. How can five hundred pounds net you a tent which is basically a carrier bag with a mesh top? I have honestly paid less than that for a car and not that many years ago either! Fortuitously, I find the model of tent that I want on eBay, second-hand but never even unwrapped. It's an American brand and someone else has had the misfortune of paying the import tax. I feel for them, but I'm well pleased with my bargain.

The choice of backpack itself is a minefield. They come

with an array of features, like built in safety whistles and loops to stow your walking poles. Some of them come with a brain, which I'm disappointed to learn has nothing to do with their intelligence…pity that. I have to decide on the capacity I need. Too big and I'll pack too much; too small and I'm just asking to get snagged on rocks and bushes with all the paraphernalia that won't fit inside it hanging off me, carabiner-ed to every available strap, tag and zip end… those carabiners weigh quite a few grams don't you know… And then you have to be fitted. There are men's and women's shapes and varying torso lengths.

Thankfully I have almost no choice whatsoever. This saves me from the very real possibility of being locked in an eternal time loop browsing Amazon and eBay, day in day out, with my brain slowly melting out through my ear holes. The shops in the UK carry hardly any of the brands available in the US. There just isn't the same hiking culture here as there is in America, and unless I want to pay a hefty import tax, I have to make the best of it. The pack I end up buying is the male model variant of the brand and capacity I want, simply because the women's equivalent isn't available in Europe yet. Surprise. Still, no worries, I have broad shoulders so it fits well. Unfortunately, it turns out that I have a "small" torso. This slight difference in height loses me three litres in capacity. Am I bitter? Yep, you bet I am! I feel cheated. That pack and I have a difficult relationship. Nothing will ever fit properly. I arrange and re-arrange my stuff for weeks. I have stern words with it to no avail; it is obstinate, awkward and petulant. In the end we come to a reluctant agreement – I ditch some of my stuff and promise not to swear at it anymore and in return it cooperates; it unlocks some hitherto unrevealed super power of pocket expansion. Peace returns.

Clothes. Who would have thought it would be so hard to pick out a simple wardrobe comprising of just one outfit, complimented by some possibly multi-purpose sleepwear? They say don't wear cotton, it doesn't wick, takes ages to dry, and chafes. I like cotton. I'm disappointed but I decide I'd better listen to the advice of Mr. Google and his friends. Merino wool is the way to go it seems. It can be worn for days and days on end without washing yourself or it and still not stink. I buy a comparatively cheap t-shirt and, as an experiment, I proceed to wear it for five days straight much to the amusement of several of my relatives. Yay. No BO. Result. I quickly follow my purchase with some merino wool pants (and I don't mean trousers if you're an American reading this!). Yes, such things do exist and they're worn by the running fraternity. The tag line printed in big letters on the waist band of this particular brand reads: "Don't run commando". The thought has never even crossed my mind until this very moment…I *could* shave off a few more grams if I…no! no! no! That really is a step too far, an open invitation to every blood sucking six-legged parasite in existence to make a beeline for my nether regions. Not going to happen! What no one tells you about merino wool, though, is that although it keeps body odour at bay, it does seem to have its own distinct fragrance. I am perturbed by the slight possibility that I may be stalked by a cougar mistakenly following the radiating scent of warm and sweaty sheep.

Whilst we're on the subject of smells, let me tell you about my quilt. This I *do* import from the States. I'm a big girl and I can't bear the thought of being zipped into a mummy bag that I might have to fight my way out of in the middle of the night to have a pee. I also have visions of being boiled alive in the summer, compounded by the fact that as a woman of a certain age even the arctic in a bikini is occasionally going to be too hot for me. On the flip side I really don't want to die of hypothermia in minus three-degree temperatures at night. So, what's to do? I settle on a ten-degree (Fahrenheit) quilt. It's going to keep me toastie warm in the spring and I can do the whole 'stick one leg out' thing to get the perfect temperature as the summer progresses. It's duck down, light and fluffy…and smelly. It takes me some time before I identify the unique odour as poultry. This smell is magnified, at least to begin with, by my also duck down booties which I wear at night to keep my toes from falling off through frost bite.

Continuing the theme of unsavoury fragrances, I might as well mention my pee-rag, some call them "pandanas". It's all very well for men, they just find a tree, aim, shake off the drips and there we go – job done. Not quite as easy for us ladies. You have to bear in mind that there are no trash cans on the trail so everything you take in you take back out with you. That includes toilet paper. Even if you choose to carry the bio-degradable stuff and bury it, the weight consideration previously mentioned rears its ugly head again. Why take reams of tissue when you can have just one small square of material that you re-use time and time again? And what do you do with your rag in the mean time? Why, you hang it off your backpack to dry in the sun of course, keeping it in easy reach for that next comfort break moment. Yes people, I kid you not. It's a thing.

I purchase another piece of bathroom equipment too, the "Deuce of Spades". A nifty little trowel made of light weight titanium with a serrated edge that's just perfect for digging little 'cat holes'; what a very appropriate term.

Then there's the question of what to do with my food. There are going to be stretches of at the very least three days, sometimes a lot longer than that, when I won't be anywhere near a service station, much less a supermarket. The calories I need are going to have to be stored and transported. Bears are a problem on some sections of the trail; they will hunt down any tasty or unusual smells and come looking for the source. They're able to detect odours far more efficiently than any domestic dog and they don't give up easily. I know. I've seen it with my own eyes. I once watched one of our bears at the park sniff out a small amount of peanut butter hidden deep in the hollow of a log. He proceeded to shred this substantial piece of wood, almost to sawdust, in less than half an hour. He didn't stop until there was absolutely no chance that there was even a molecule of spread left behind.

There are two schools of thought on how to tackle this issue and both camps are pretty passionate about their methods. You can hang your food from a tree in a bag, either a strong waterproof bag, similar to those used by kayakers, or a purpose manufactured bear bag. The disadvantage with this method is that one needs to find a suitable tree with just the right branch, at the just the right angle, and just the right distance from the ground and the trunk. And then one has to accurately throw a rope, weighted with a reasonably sized stick or some such heavy object, over the said branch. The hope is that it doesn't ricochet off anything on the way up, or come to that on the way down…like, for example, a human head. I can't imagine anything more time consumingly arduous at the end of a long day's hiking.

The other faction supports the use of a bear barrel. This is basically what it says on the label - a super strong plastic barrel with a fiendishly difficult to open lid, even for species with opposable thumbs. Especially, I discover later, when it's cold. You put your food and ALL the other potentially smellable items inside, then place it between fifty and two hundred feet from your tent somewhere you can find it again. The bear shouldn't be able to smell the contents, but even if it does come across the thing and decides to roll it around it's tough enough to withstand bear teeth and claws.

I pick the second option. I reckon it'll be a lot less hassle. Besides, I have realistic expectations of my rope tossing potential; the barrel will probably save me from concussion or the odd black eye. Anyway, it'll double up as a camp seat. Momentarily I remember how enthusiastically our bears would play with floating logs and beef knuckle bones and picture my barrel rolling down a cliff, floating away in a river, or lost forever buried under a few feet of leaf litter. On balance, I conclude it's still the better option so I stick to my decision.

Every piece of equipment and every item of clothing becomes a minefield of deliberation. It all boils down to cost versus weight. I love good coffee but I reluctantly ditch the idea of taking any kind of brewing device; none of them are small enough, light enough or cheap enough, and coffee grounds weigh more than sachets of instant. Then there's the question of what to do with the grounds. The "Leave No Trace" purists won't scatter or bury them. Am *I* prepared to pack them out? There are some things I'm not prepared to compromise on though. I plan to vlog on YouTube as I'm convinced that no one will believe I'm actually there, and that everyone secretly thinks I've booked into a luxury spa resort for half a year. To this end, I've bought a pretty decent camera that does selfie videoing. The problem is that it weighs five hundred grams! The 'ultra-lite police' might as well handcuff me right now.

I plan to journal every day and I have a long debate with myself about the virtues of a tablet versus good old-fashioned notebook and pencil. The first means extra weight in the form of an additional powerpack *and* it's breakable, the second is extra weight in the form of paper. A bit of research turns up a brand of waterproof pads and pens and I opt for these. I reason that they're not going to break, they won't disintegrate if I'm unfortunate enough to fall into a river or get caught in a storm, and I can always take photos of the individual pages on my mobile phone for paranoia's sake.

I have a moment of uncharacteristic sensibleness, and I decide to purchase a GPS device, mostly so the people back home can track my progress on a map displayed on a web page that they can log into. Again - that spa resort thing. It's tiny and it's light. It also comes with a promise: should I fall off a cliff, get eaten by a bear, or become hopelessly lost as a result of heat stroke or hypothermia induced delirium, they will find and rescue me, or retrieve my body parts and send them home. There are a couple of problems with this. Firstly, one must take out a subscription, a disproportionately expensive subscription…I guess they're anticipating the cost of scrambling that fleet of helicopters. Secondly, one has to press an SOS button if one is in trouble. This, I imagine, is not easy if you are tumbling down a ravine or are having your arms chewed off by that bear, more so as this *very* small button is hidden under a hard to remove plastic flap designed to prevent accidental activation. Useful? You decide. Then, should I be able to negotiate this thoughtful little design feature immediately prior to the aforementioned bear chewing off the aforementioned arm, which may well be holding the aforementioned GPS device, my rescue party will very successfully find the afore-aforementioned bear, who by this time will be in need of veterinary treatment for severe indigestion having swallowed the whole lot. I decide I'm clearly overthinking the entire thing and I just part with my bank details.

Another sensible bit of kit that I invest in is my tick lasso. Ticks are a big thing out there, in fact, they're becoming a big thing here too. There's even a warning poster on the notice board at my local woods in Kent. It's not the tick as such that is the problem, although no one really wants to have what's described as an "ectoparasitic arachnid" bury its, to quote the Wiki, "feeding structure with mouthparts adapted for piercing skin and sucking blood" into their flesh, and watch as it slowly swells into a globular grey wart. Even the words "feeding structure" are enough to send shivers up my spine. My imagination has already conjured up images of zoonotic DNA mutations, like the script of "The Fly" or some other bad b-movie from the fifties. Anyway, back in reality…its actually the microorganisms in the tick saliva that *should* send one into a cold sweat. If the tick becomes traumatised in the process of removal it will vomit into the open wound that its "feeding structure" has dug, allowing whatever bacteria it's carrying to enter into your bloodstream. The most well-known of these is the cause of Lyme disease, which can result in serious and debilitating physical symptoms. It is relatively easy to cure if it's caught in a small time-window of a few months after a bite is noticed. The trouble is that a huge percentage of people never know they were bitten, and even in those people who do notice a bite, the tell-tale bulls-eye rash doesn't always appear despite them having been infected. The trick to avoiding this whole skin crawling scenario is to remove the tick within a couple of days and to do it very, very, carefully. Treat the little beasty gently and keep it from trauma and it won't puke. The tick lasso goes around the base of the body and tightens up, then with one elegant twist and an upward pull it comes free before it even has the time to look for a sick bucket. Take home message – be nice to your tick and get rid of it quick.

Eventually I draw up a kit list, acquire most of the items on it, squeeze them into my not quite big enough by three litres backpack, and hope for the best.

CHAPTER TWO

The Beginning - a steep (ha-ha) learning curve.

Well, I'm on the plane. No going back then. The start of my epic journey, one that will no doubt take me somewhere north of my comfort zone. I suspect it'll be a journey not just in the physical sense, but I guess an emotional and spiritual one too. This notion starts to materialise into reality quite soon. As I gaze out of the window, I can see the shadow of my plane beautifully silhouetted and clearly defined on the surface of the deep blue ocean water below, and it reminds me of the last plane journey my dad and I took together. We were flying home from Hungary after a week of visiting relatives. It was a kind of 'goodbye trip'. Dad had pretty advanced leukaemia by then. I'd spent a lot of the trip not feeling great myself and he ended up looking out for me more than I did for him. I guess it was nice for him to know he was still needed, that it made no difference that he was ill, he was still my dad and I'd let him be just that, no matter what. To me he was still strong. He had an amazing ability to just ignore any hardship or personal limitation and plough on through regardless with the most remarkable determination. Whatever it was, he'd get it done and he'd do it with the minimum amount of fuss. He was still driving his car the day before he died, I have no idea where that kind of grit comes from. Nothing stopped him, only death itself finally managed that. I remember him marvelling at how miraculous the ability to travel above the clouds seemed. Science fascinated him; I think he'd have loved to take a trip into space if he'd ever been given the opportunity. I remember him pointing out to me all the towns and villages passing by below us. It had made me feel like a little girl again. The memory feels just a day old and not the twelve years that it's been in reality. Sitting on this plane I'm suddenly surprised as I realise that I still miss him, and I try not to let my emotions overflow; I hate crying in public.

I'm struck by the juxtaposition between my current and future modes of transportation. Right now, I'm utilising one of mankind's most technologically advanced achievements – the ability to fly, but soon I'm going to be heading into the backwoods to live like a stone age person. Well…not exactly *that* primitive, what with all the expensive lightweight equipment I'm packing, but to be fair my ancestors from deep time didn't need half the paraphernalia that I think is necessary for survival. They had the skills to make what they needed. I wonder to myself on the likelihood that they ever whittled a spork…

I land at Washington Dulles. I've only ever passed through the States to change planes and I've never been out of the American airports that I've visited, so this is all a bit of a culture shock to me. I didn't realise Washington DC had three airports until a few weeks ago, and it takes me a fair while to find out that the 'DC' stands for District of Columbia.

As I walk along the edge of a busy road to the nearest supermarket for my first supply stop, I come to the realisation that 'sidewalk' really is just that and not a bad translation of 'pavement'. There's a white line marking the boundary between vehicular and pedestrian territory. That's it. No curb. No change in the surface material. Nothing. Just the line. The next few weeks will teach me that the obsession we seem to have with health and safety doesn't appear to be shared by the Americans - as far as my experience goes at any rate. I notice that the trucks seem colossal compared to what I'm used to seeing on British roads, their cabs look big enough to set up home in. I figure there wouldn't be much of me left if I end up plastered to the front bumper of one of them, so I opt for the grass verge wherever I can. At one point I have to step around the remains of what appears to be some kind of large ungulate in an advanced state of decay. I'm grateful that I paid attention to the osteology module during my recently achieved degree because it enables me to know beyond a shadow of a doubt that the bones which I'm looking at are definitely not from a two-legged creature. A bit further on there's a ripe, and much more recently deceased racoon. Well, let's be positive here – at least I've seen some native wildlife on my first day, although I was rather hoping that my first encounter with the indigenous species would be a bit more animated!

Any disappointment quickly fades away as I enter the supermarket. They have Nutella in plastic jars and Snyder's pretzels in my all-time favourite flavour – buffalo hot wing! I haven't been able to find these particular ones in England for ages now. There's instant mashed potato in a choice of exciting varieties and tuna in sachets! I'm like a pig in muck. I have no idea what the locals doing their weekly shop must be thinking about this crazy English woman. There's a fixed grin on my face as I dive in and out of the aisles in a state of euphoric excitement like I've just been released from a decade of incarceration in some institution or other. I have to say though that my most exciting food discovery didn't happen until quite a few weeks later when I found that Spam came in single serve packets. I could hardly contain myself!

There's something amazingly satisfying about being an overweight, middle-aged woman scrutinizing the back of food packets to find the maximum number of calories packed into the minimum number of grams. I've spent good money on Weight Watchers programmes in the past and this activity makes me feel like a rebellious, naughty kid…but in a strangely self-righteous way. One of the highlights of my first week becomes eating Nutella straight out of the jar. Coincidentally, this particular brand of chocolate and hazelnut spread also becomes an accidental thermometer too. I learn to gauge the outside temperature just by the consistency of the spread: the harder it is to scrape the stuff out with my spork the closer it is to freezing; chipping it out in tiny bits means it's dropped into minus figures.

I congratulate myself on squeezing all my new found delights into my bear barrel, no mean feat I can tell you! To save space I've thrown away all the redundant packaging; there was as much of that as there was actual food. I feel assured that whatever horrors the trail chooses to throw at me starvation won't be one of them…at least not for the first five days.

I take an Uber to Harpers Ferry, West Virginia. This is another first for me. I've never used the service before and I only downloaded the app to my smartphone recently. It's an extra expense but I decide that I'm not brave enough to hitchhike, besides, it's illegal in some States to do that. As the weeks go by, I end up having some interesting conversations with the drivers who ferry me to and from the trail to re-supply and zero (a day off from walking). They are an eclectic array of diverse characters, each with a unique story. Mostly they are friendly, but there's the odd ones who're so precious about their cars that they all but have a coronary when I so much as try to touch their vehicle with my dirty hiker hands to open the trunk and deposit my malodorous backpack into it. Probably not an unreasonable reaction, I guess.

Back in the day, a guy called Robert Harper ran a ferry across the river here - hence the name of the place, although somewhere along the line it did officially lose its apostrophe. The place has a lot of Civil War history. The railway and canal that run through the town linked Washington to the west of America as well as providing an access route between the States in the north and those in the south. It was a geographic intersection point making it a strategically handy place to control, and it was the Confederate army's most northern stronghold. I guess it's most famous for John Brown, whose raid on the town armoury rather fatally failed in 1859…but at least they wrote a song about him – ok, so it was about his mouldering body but being immortalised forevermore is still quite an achievement for something that went wrong…bit like good old Guy Fawkes I suppose.

The Appalachian Trail Conservancy (ATC) headquarters is located just off mile 1025.5 of the trail itself, and I've come here to register my thru-hike. I'm doing what they call a Flip-Flop, so I'm basically starting my journey here and walking north, then returning to Harpers Ferry to complete my trek by walking the remainder in a southernly direction. The Conservancy are encouraging thru-hikers to take this route to mitigate the amount of damage done by the sheer volume of footfall caused by the large number of thru-hikers all starting from Springer Mountain in Georgia at around about the same time each year. This sizable group of people is known as "The Bubble" and, apart from the actual damage it causes to the path, it's also resulted in competition for tent sites and shelter space as it moves up the trail. A vast majority of those that start quit after the first couple of weeks, so the greatest impact is at the beginning. Encouraging people to start at Harpers Ferry takes some of that pressure away.

Just inside the doorway of the building is a rather worrying notice board labelled "Hikers, know your ticks!" Apparently, this informative infographic is supplied by the "TickEncounter Resource Centre". I'm mildly alarmed by the fact that an organisation of this name even exists. There's a picture of four different varieties of tick in all stages of their development, annotated with the names of no less than ten different diseases they carry between them. Not the reassuring welcome I was hoping for. But, to be fair, one of those ticks is only the humble dog tick which transmits exactly zero of those nasty viruses so I only have to worry about the other three...this doesn't make me feel a whole lot better. How I'm going to tell the difference when my only close up view of one of these is probably going to be its tiny butt sticking out of my skin is beyond me; they're all just eight legged brownish-orange creepy looking things. But, nevertheless, I consider myself informed. The powers that be have done their job and I can't say that I haven't been warned.

A member of staff takes my picture next to the wall outside under the conservancy sign and AT logo, gives me a number, and puts my photo in the book. It's March so this year's book only has just over a dozen other smiley happy hikers' mugshots preceding mine, I guess that will have increased to hundreds by the time I'm back here again in July. Another worker, Mountain Laurel a veteran thru-hiker, has a friendly chat with me. Reading between the lines, I think she's checking out whether I know what I'm letting myself in for; her questions make me think she's on a mission to weed out those under-prepared hikers that might not realise that they are heading off into the woods on a suicide mission. I pass muster. That's it, all official now. The journey 'proper' begins.

I start off a day earlier than I had intended to so that I can avoid the possibility of getting caught up in the rain that's been forecast for tomorrow. As I walk out of the town the people that I pass ask me questions like "Where have you come from?" and "How far are you going?" I have to think carefully about the answers that I give them. Have I come from the South East of England, the United Kingdom, Washington DC? Am I going to Maine, Maryland, as far as I can get before dark? What are they asking? What do they want to know? Do *they* even know? It strikes me that it's all about the asker's viewpoint, and mine too. I start to wonder about the conversations we have every day that rely on the assumptions we make about one another's perspectives. How many misunderstandings must go completely unnoticed until, somewhere down the line, we find ourselves with broken friendships and marriages; not realising the gradual steps along the way where we missed the true meaning behind the words that we exchanged with each other, gradually building into insurmountable walls between us... In retrospect that's probably metaphysical overkill - the townsfolk were probably only trying to make friendly, light conversation.

The first few miles are a dream. The bridge I take, which is situated at the confluence of the Shenandoah and Potomac rivers, is covered by meshed ironwork and there are numerous padlocks hanging along its length. Some of them are placed in locations that must have been insanely dangerous to reach. I guess the lovers who locked them in place probably imagined that the degree of their devotion to each other was directly proportional to the danger they were prepared to put themselves in. It would have been a bit rough if they'd died in the process, but they say that love is blind and I guess that includes blind to common sense too. By the time I step off at the other end, I have crossed into Maryland. It's weeks before I find out why people laugh at me every time I talk about this State. Apparently "Mary Land" is actually pronounced "Maralind" - who knew? I can see my first white blaze up ahead, and the trail continues dead flat for a while, sharing this section with the Chesapeake and Ohio canal towpath. I'm thinking to myself that this is good, 2192 miles of this will be a breeze. The blatantly obvious fact that the Appalachian Trail follows the Appalachian Mountain range has somehow failed to register in my head. I'm expecting hills, even steep hills...and the odd stone, even a rock or two maybe. I'm in for a rude awakening it turns out. I guess the clue was in the name...and the tiny little statistic that I must have glossed over in my research - the gains and losses in elevation along the trail's length are equivalent to climbing the highest mountain in the world, Everest, sixteen times.

After three miles the trail leaves the towpath and starts to climb. It becomes very narrow and I'm walking close to the edge of a sheer drop with lots of vindictive looking tree roots stealthily scheming ways to ensnare my ankles and send me plummeting to an untimely grave. I'm wishing that I'd practiced flipping the cover off that SOS button now, you know…just in case. I thank God for my decision to leave early; in tomorrow's rain this path will be a skiddy mud slick. I hate heights and there aren't even any leaves on the trees this time of year to hide the altogether too clear of a view all the way to the bottom. What am I doing exactly? Maybe my mother was right in thinking I've taken leave of my senses coming here? Maybe some self-destructive streak in my psyche has won over my rational thought processes? There's 'testing your mettle' and then there is 'suicide mission'…perhaps the line between the two is closer and more blurred than one might think! It turns out that this slightly panic inducing start is going to be one of the tamer offerings the AT will dish up for me in the next few months. Again – who knew? Anyway, I survive the evil roots and the vertiginous path and even see a White-tailed deer. Yay! Actual living wildlife! I arrive at the Ed Garvey shelter where I stay the night.

What can I say about the shelters on the AT? Basically, they are three-sided structures open to the elements on one side. Why this side is always facing the prevailing wind baffles me. There's an internal platform off the ground that's designed to house multiple people on their sleeping mats. They're mostly made like log cabins but some have solid sides and a few are even fully enclosed. They vary in size and quality, some are extremely well kept, elaborate with thoughtful touches like ornaments, some have basic bunks, some have an 'upstairs' area too. They all have a log book. The idea is that you write a little something either about your stay, a message for friends coming up behind you on the trail, news of the terrain for travellers coming from the opposite direction, or something existentially philosophical if the mood takes you. I guess, should you go missing, it is also a point of reference for your rescuers in terms of setting a search grid. There is usually an area around the shelter suitable for tenting, and more often than not there's a basic privy close by.

It's cold enough for hypothermia to be a real threat tonight so I do a 'naughty' and erect my tent inside the shelter. This is absolutely definitely bad etiquette and is frowned upon. I reason that it's so early in the season and so late in the day that no one else is going to be arriving here tonight in any case. I'm pretty glad I do though because during the night I hear trees crashing to the ground nearby and in the morning the area is littered with a tangled mess of twigs and branches. It's weeks later that I find out about a guy who was killed by a falling tree very near to here in 2015…probably just as well I didn't know about that at the time.

The promised rain arrives the next day as predicted. The weather app on my phone flashes up a flood warning for this area. I put my tent up inside the shelter again and go to bed. It's a cold and wet night at the Crampton Gap shelter and I'm in absolute disbelief when a couple turn up at eleven thirty that night by the light of their head torches. That's crazy ramped up to a whole new level! Thankfully there's enough room for them around my tent and I feign sleep so I don't have to get into the whole "I'm sorry I pitched my tent in here but I really didn't think there was a snowball's chance in hell anyone would be insane enough to be wandering around in the dark in a rain storm in the middle of nowhere at this time of night in the woods" conversation. I'm relieved to find that they're gone by the time I wake up in the morning.

I look around and for some reason I start singing "Islands in the stream" in my head as I regard the multiple rivulets between me and the path to the privy. What was I expecting? A patio and decking? A canoe would have been nice though. I also learn that the shelters have other residents than humans; my pot cosy is chewed and all my gear smells of rodent. Nice.

I have a bit of time in the morning so I write in my journal and reflect. I'm thinking it's amazing what a human being (me) can achieve when there's no other choice. When I have to put one foot in front of the other regardless of how far out of my comfort zone I am. My universe has reduced down into the space immediately in front of me, neither to one side nor to the other. Just then. Just there. Just in front. One more step, and one more, and one more. Only that next step exists. Only the very next step matters. It feels like mindfulness on steroids. It's amazing what a human being (me) can bear. Maybe we're all a lot more tenacious than we imagine, maybe all it requires is a series of events to test the mettle of our (my) capabilities to bring that tenacity out of hiding. Mud. Rocks. Height. Cold. Wind and rain. The sound of branches crashing down in the night. A coyote howl in the dark. None of it I'm comfortable with, but I'm adapting nonetheless. My idea of what I need, what is acceptable, is being honed now that I'm literally just interested in survival. Everything comes down to a sharp point of focus. I'm filtering out the extraneous so I don't waste my energy on it. One purpose: get through the days and nights and don't die. All else seems to matter a whole lot less. Never mind tomorrow, forget about yesterday. Now. Right now.

Everything's a bit damp and my toes are really cold in my wet socks and boots. The sun comes out a bit as I walk the quarter of a mile up a steep slope back to the trail on saturated ground.

My third night out and I'm tenting at the Dahlgren campsite. There are showers here but of course they're all locked up as the season proper hasn't started yet. Still, the privy is an actual Portaloo with a trash can. This is a real treat because all my garbage has to be packed out so I relish any opportunity to dump what I've collected so far. There's a forecast for thunder at 4am tonight and I've had to pitch under some dodgy looking trees. I'm concerned enough to WhatsApp some friends back home to pray I make it out alive by the morning without being pancaked in the night.

The question of where exactly is safe to camp in terms of widow-maker branches and standing deadwood arises again and again as I progress on my journey. The best answer I can get from the seasoned local camping fraternity is that if I'm not dead in the morning I chose well…hardly reassuring. Everywhere along the trail there is evidence of wind damage. The remains of substantially sized trees in varying states of decay are strewn on either side of the path, many have fallen across it and have had sections chain sawed out to permit passage. I guess the mountain sides are steep or exposed allowing the wind to whip through, uprooting trees easily from the shallow layer of top soil that sits on the rock below.

It's snowing ever so slightly. My stove is taking ages to boil the water that's needed to reconstitute my supper. Apparently, this happens in the cold; stoves become less efficient. And yet again – who knew? Despite the time of year and the weather there are other people at the campsite tonight. One guy's camped with his daughter. He tells me that he leads a Nazarene church. I have no idea what that is and I've only heard the word in association with John the Baptist. I curtail the ridiculous sense of humour that always bubbles up in me when I'm tired and, with difficulty, I refrain from asking him if he's got a couple of locusts that he could spare to liven up my dinner as I've heard that insects are high in protein.

The wind gets up in the night but I don't get squashed and no trees fall over or lose any limbs. It is cold though. The temperature drops to minus one and I'm forced to wear all my clothes including my rain trousers, puffy jacket and balaclava, but it's much worse outside my tent, so when I realise that I need to pee I'm faced with a bit of a dilemma. I spend what seems like an eternity trying to decide whether my bladder will make it till the morning. I conclude that it'll probably explode if I don't stop messing about and address the issue soon. My tent has two vestibules under the fly sheet, so I unzip my inner tent to access the one I was planning on using should ever there arise the kind of emergency that might involve not being able to use the entrance proper, like a bear poking its head in, for example. After performing some kind of ridiculously undignified pseudo-yoga manoeuvre that involves removing just enough clothing to stand a reasonable chance of relieving myself without getting soaked, *and* having a fleeting moment of panic when I realise that if I end up getting cramp (which is actually a real possibility after days of walking) this whole plan will be a damp and painful failure, I achieve my goal successfully…but only just. Who knew a bathroom break could require so much planning and thought? Now I know that it's doable, it becomes a terrible habit I employ in the future when it's raining at night.

On the subject of peeing…every tree along the trail is a potential public convenience and one must choose wisely when and which to utilise. There will be times ahead when I misjudge this and narrowly escape flashing my behind at unsuspecting day hikers who are walking their dogs and their children. That said, it is amazing how quickly I cease to care who sees my butt or where I pee, it's also amazing how fast I learn to pee quickly.

The terrain is much better the next day despite the elevation changes. There's a bit more mud but a few less rocks and its sunny and warm. I cross over a road and pass by a stone church that looks as if it would be right at home in my neck of the woods in Kent. It's got a little steeple with a stone cross on the top. A mile or so on, I stop at the Washington Monument State Park. The monument was the first one built to commemorate George Washington himself. It was erected by the villagers of Boonsboro to celebrate Independence Day on the fourth of July 1827. The building's shape kind of reminds me of an old-fashioned honey pot, tapering slightly towards the apex with a flat top that looks like the lid.

I continue to walk on another seven miles. There are a lot of logs to climb over on the trail. I eventually pull into camp at Pogo Memorial Campsite. It's a tent site in an actual forest and the pitches are few, far between and not particularly level. I literally end up having to crawl uphill out of my tent to pee in the night. This isn't made any easier by the fact that my legs have kept cramping up often and unexpectedly since I laid down. The privy is out of site and I won't risk trying to find it in the dark. Once, whilst camping in the New Forest in Hampshire, England, when my kids were young, I actually got lost coming back from the toilet block on the camp site and ended up wandering around for nearly an hour before I finally spotted my car and my tent. I really don't want a repeat of that in the deep woods of America - It's too early days to be testing out that SOS button. However, despite all that, I sleep well enough.

As I walk along the trail in the morning, the shallow puddles of water that have frozen in the night crackle with each footstep. They're a montage of the local flora, like a child's collage after a nature walk, the copious quantities of PVA glue holding the leaves together replaced by clear ice instead. Nine miles today. Nine miles of what I consider to be hell. I discover that the phrase "a bit rocky" has been lost in translation somewhere in the middle of the Atlantic Ocean. To me "a bit rocky" might imply that there are a few stones the size of rockery rocks strewn across the path every so often, like in a fancy bit of garden design maybe. It turns out that "a bit rocky" actually means fields of boulders the size of kitchen cabinets, washing machines and microwave ovens roughly thrown randomly together along ridge lines with not inconsiderable drops either side. Not for the last time I'm shell shocked at what constitutes a "trail" in this country. I congratulate myself for keeping my s**t together and not dying.

At one point in the day the terrain eases into something I might consider normal and I run across a family walking their dachshunds on a grassy field. They assure me that I'm not far from the state line now, maybe ten miles, and that the worst of Maryland is over. I'm inclined to believe them because there's no chance dogs with legs that short have been walked over the kind of terrain I've been on today – they'd fall down the cracks between the slabs of rock and disappear into the depths of Hades in a heartbeat. I'm really glad to hear this favourable info as there's about a gnat's pee chance in hell that I'm going to get to camp before dark. I could cry from relief.

…They lied. There's a cold and fast flowing river. It's between me and the camp site and there's no bridge. If I dally for even one second, I know I'm going to bottle it, so I literally wade through the thing trying to balance on the barely visible stones under the surface and my boots gradually fill up with water. I don't fall in though, which is just as well as I realise my phone isn't in its waterproof bag and my gear in my backpack isn't either. I have to sit down on the other side and pour the water out of my boots and wring out my socks before putting them back on again to continue up a very long and very steep hill. Near the top a terribly 'helpful' young man filling up his water bottle from a mini waterfall announces in an encouraging voice that the shelter is "just around the corner". I guess he can see I'm not having the best day I've ever attempted to live through. Well, he's clearly either insanely optimistic or corners are very, very long in this country. Finally, I stagger into Raven Rock shelter. I erect my tent in the dark, and then I have to walk a third of a mile down a steep and slippery hill by the light of my head torch on a sketchily marked blue blazed trail to fetch water from the nearest spring. I ache all over. It has been, by a long chalk, the worst day so far. Thankfully my tent is on a soft gravelly platform that's comfy to sleep on and it's a bit warmer tonight.

I notice I'm getting a bit quicker at the knock down in the mornings. There's one way everything fits…well, sort of fits. As I mentioned before, my backpack and I don't have the best relationship in the entire world, it's a weird shape with these extra little bits tucked around the side in the bottom of the main compartment. I can't imagine anything that'd fit in there usefully. They're about the right size for a fat hamster. I didn't bring one of those, not even for an emergency snack, on the grounds that the 'ultra-lite police' would lock me up and throw away the key. Before I leave, I go over and chat to a guy, Pilgrim, who slept in the shelter last night. He's decided to stay put for the day to avoid the coming rain. He's walking with no plan or agenda, just pottering along the trail.

In some ways, everything has slowed down for me too. It's as though time is almost still. Everything is drawn out, taking longer, methodical. I have to think carefully about all the individual steps required to complete each simple activity. Going to the toilet, making a coffee, getting ready for bed. Each is a long process. Thought slows me down. I begin to notice the background noise of life, it becomes louder; I hear the wind moving the leaves in the trees, the water running over the rocks, the rustling in the undergrowth as birds forage for insects. The foreground noises associated with busy modern life fade and slip to one side as I live each individual moment, and there is thankfulness for each of those moments of life. I am present. I am here. I am 'now'.

I'm learning that a positive mental attitude helps with the demands that the trail puts on me. I tell myself that these are not rocks, they are steps. If they weren't here, I wouldn't be able to get up this mountainside. And that I'm nearly at the top when in reality I'm only a quarter of the way up a hill. I'm thankful that there will be water and that I know where it is, rather than focussing on how far away it is and how hard it will be to collect. My legs burn, but I concentrate on the fact that I actually have legs and that they are still working, and how amazing the human body is. There is a mantra constantly running through my head: "One step, just one step, one step, this step, just one step."

CHAPTER THREE

Turns out Pilgrim had the right idea.

I walk in the rain all day. I make another discovery – waterproofs are not actually waterproof; they are water *resistant*. I find that the willingness of my particular waterproofs to resist is seriously lacking. I secretly wonder if they are in cahoots with my ornery backpack, colluding and conspiring together for nefarious ends. To compound it all, the trail seems to have become a bit of a suggestion. Time and again I see a white blaze in the distance and I have to find my own way to it over boulders with alarmingly deep and jagged spaces in between. One miss-step and I'm sure that at best I'll bust an ankle or at worst puncture an artery.

Eventually I reach Penn-Mar State Park. It's like a ghost town and there isn't even an open toilet block to use so I resort to peeing in a sheltered corner at the foot of the raised pavilion where I have my lunch. Well, it's not like there's anyone out in this cold wet weather to catch a glimpse of my bare behind…you'd think, wouldn't you? A girl out for a jog passes by, thankfully oblivious. I am flabbergasted to see that she's in tiny shorts, hardly bigger than underwear, and a t-shirt. I, on the other hand, have several layers of clothing on and am still pretty well chilled to the bone. I try to look on the bright side though and admire the view from the pavilion over the surrounding countryside, it's spectacular, or at least it would be if it wasn't obscured by mist and cloud…I fill in the blanks with my imagination.

Finally, I'm over the Mason-Dixon Line and across into Pennsylvania! One State down, thirteen to go. Forty-two miles clocked up. Goodbye Maryland! I feel epic and decide to celebrate by Ubering to a motel. The driver is very gracious despite the fact that I have now not showered or washed my clothes for six days. My pungent aroma has not been helped by the fact that I opted to leave my deodorant at home too…those extra grams.

I decide to have a proper zero as the temperatures have dropped down to 'chip the Nutella with an ice pick' cold out there and I feel like I've been on a cross trainer for six days solid. For two nights I'm living in luxury. Finally, I'm clean and warm. It is truly amazing. I find out that most motels seem to have climate control, microwaves, fridges and guest laundry facilities as standard. The laundry is basically one top loading washing machine (I thought these went out with the ark, but apparently this news hasn't gone global yet) and one tumble dryer. These machines always seem to be located on another floor than the room I'm staying in…bit of a logistical nightmare if everything you own is dirty. My routine on hitting a town on the occasions when I stay at a motel runs something like this: Purchase seriously overpriced laundry detergent from reception. Straight into my room. Strip. Empty backpack all over the bed. Hit the shower. (I'm so thankful for the free teeny-weeny shampoo, teeny-weeny block of soap and, if I am very, very lucky, teeny-weeny conditioner. You know - the ones that somehow seem to 'accidentally' end up coming home in your suitcase after a holiday.) Stuff all my clothes into a couple of spare dry sacks. Dress in my waterproof trousers and my puffy jacket. Run barefoot down the corridor, into the elevator, back down another corridor and bung the contents of my bags into the washer, praying that no one has seen me. This whole embarrassing expedition is repeated twice more to swap the clothes into the dryer and then to retrieve them again. A two-hour period of feeling seriously disconcerted, vulnerable, and semi-naked, hoping desperately that no one will steal my entire wardrobe whilst I'm away from it. On one occasion I order take out and the delivery guy has no idea where to look as he waits for me to pay; I'm standing in what looks to all intents and purposes like some kind of dodgy 'fifty shades of flasher-mac' outfit. I can almost see the thoughts running through his head as he wonders who I've got in there with me and exactly what it is that we might be up to. I recall all those customers I used to deliver food to and am now, myself, thankful I'm never going to meet this guy again. Ever.

Another thing that's standard is paper crockery and plastic cutlery. I can't quite believe what it is that I'm seeing at first, and I chalk it up to the fact I'm in a cheap establishment. But no, every motel I stay in has this throw away culture. What is that all about? Do Americans break a disproportionately large number of plates and cups? Perhaps washing dishes just isn't a thing here? The entire aisle given over to disposable table wear in every Walmart that I've been in now makes sense. Mind you, after finding out that gravy in this country is white and thick like a sauce, and that it's served with 'biscuits' that are quite clearly scones, nothing should surprise me anymore!

I get some routine housekeeping of my own done. I manage to shop smarter at the local supermarket this time, squeezing even more calories into even less space. I discover Lara bars, they're a kind of chewy bar made from just squished down nuts, dried fruit and nothing else. I've heard people raving about them so I buy a few to see what the fuss is all about. They turn out to taste quite nice. Parmesan crisps are another winner. Incredibly light, incredibly tasty, and incredibly full of fat.

I charge up all my electronics whilst I'm here and then

wrestle with a 'simple' piece of software on my phone to produce a half-way to decent vlog which I upload to my YouTube channel, "On Wings Like Eagles". This is also the trail name I have adopted for now (more about that later). Yay for free Wi-Fi! I toy with the idea of shopping for a head camera online as I don't think the footage that I've shot so far even begins to approach doing justice to the reality of 'a bit rocky'. I also think it might make me braver if I'm motivated to capture the true essence of why having a limited stock of underwear may be a significant gamble on this terrain. I shelve the idea in favour of making a bonus video that I pretentiously call "Thought for the week".

In the evening I visit a nearby diner. I'm amused to see that the slogan on the paper napkins reads "No Sweat". Appropriate…first time in six days. I order a bottle of root beer; it's got to be one of my favourite fizzy drinks. Back in the day, McDonald's used to sell it in the UK, ok it did taste a bit like toothpaste but I was still gutted when they took it off the menu. The one I have with my meal has nothing 'toothpastey' about it at all. It's amazing. Heaven in a glass bottle.

I head out the next morning via the local post office. There's an elderly man in there joking with the staff. It seems to me like he's probably a regular because the ladies behind the counter refer to him as the "Candy Man". This is not, thankfully, alluding to the American slasher movie of the same name but refers to actual candy, as in sweets. He squeezes two Werther's Originals into my hand with a lovely smile on his face. I get into a conversation, not for the last time on this trip, about who I am and what I am doing. Of course, when they hear my accent, they all think I'm Australian to begin with – this is a common misconception, perhaps they don't get a lot of Aussies around these parts? Mind you, I must admit that the occasional antipodean twang in my accent has been spotted by people in Britain too. I put that down to having spent six months living in New Zealand when I was three and a half years old, still young enough to be picking up an accent. After the Candy Man hears my tale, he gives me a handful more of his candy stash and says it's "for your journey". It makes me smile and I feel so blessed and all warm and fuzzy on the inside. I tuck them into a little zip pocket on the front of my jacket and keep them for special moments when I really need a lift. They last me for a few weeks.

The rest of the day doesn't go too well. The trail markers get a bit sketchy; they are faded and badly placed. I don't get lost but I do feel disconcerted, especially when I pass by a spring where I had planned to collect water. The place feels somehow odd – I can't really put my finger on it but I feel unsettled there and decide to move on quickly. I don't mind the woods, even in the dark I'm not that bothered by them. I've always figured that I'm more likely to run into trouble in my home town on a Friday night after pub chucking out time than in the middle of nowhere. There are some places that do have a bad vibe for no obvious reason though; there's a particular spot along one of the woodland trails I used to walk between lectures at University which gave me the same irrational creepy feeling every time I went past it.

By the time I roll into camp I feel badly homesick. I'm *really* missing my people; my non-DNA family. It's a Wednesday evening, the night our homegroup meet up every week. It's a close group, honest, real, and non-judgemental, they've supported me through some difficult times and the bonds of friendship and fellowship run pretty deep. I spend a lot of time talking to God about it and I feel a bit better.

It's a cold night but it's been worse. The shelter, or should I say shelters, at Tumbling Run, are well kept. There are two. One has a little notice on the side that reads "Snoring", the other "Non-snoring". Between them is a covered area with a picnic bench, there's even a little vase with a plastic flower in it. I meet the caretaker in the morning. His name is George and he's come to check up on things. I'm left wondering whether he is a snorer or a nonsnorer. The privy is amazingly clean…not all of them are.

Most of the privies are basically an unplumbed and free-standing toilet, or in some cases a wooden box seat with a hole cut in it, situated over a pit. You do your thing and the pile below gradually grows over time so you can imagine that, clearly, they are not going to smell too great. That said, some of them have buckets of wood chippings, the idea being that you throw a handful in after you're done and the waste eventually turns into compost over time. These are known as mouldering privies. They actually smell ok. One of the first things I do when I get into camp is to check out the privy. Some of them are big enough to house a troop of boy scouts and are sufficiently weather tight to afford emergency shelter in a storm. I reckon I'd have to be pretty desperate though! Some of them I probably couldn't swing an average sized gerbil in, and then there are those that make me turn around, shut the door and head for a suitable tree with my Deuce of Spades at the ready.

Later, I meet two hikers from Hawaii coming southbound and stop to have a chat. I forget to ask them their names. It turns out they've been staying in motels a lot to avoid the cold weather. I guess being used to living in mid Pacific temperatures has made it difficult for them to acclimatise. They do mention one shelter that they reckon is worth a visit though, they describe it as the "Disneyland of shelters". I'm intrigued. The guy has had a bit of a fall and repaired his trousers with tenacious tape. I mentally congratulate myself for including it in my meagre repertoire of supplies after reading reports of its almost miraculously reparative properties. Apparently, looking at the evidence standing before me, it does in fact do what it says on the tin, a rare attribute these days. I'm also slightly apprehensive that if this fit, athletic and balanced looking bloke managed to lose his footing on the rocks that I have yet to traverse up ahead, how am I going to fare?

There's a tiny little side trail with the promise of a view so I take it. I do my first proper rock climbing where I have to stow my poles…over, like, three rocks. There's a lady at the top nonchalantly sitting a lot closer to the edge than I'd be comfortable with. She offers to take my photo with the illusion of an insane drop in the background and I pass her my camera, thinking how 'bad ass' it's going to make me look.

One positive thing I will say about Pennsylvania is that it might be rocky but there are some pretty spectacular views just off the trail, and often a nice little rocky outcrop to sit on and enjoy them. Every so often there are also good views where cuts through the woods have been made to accommodate power or gas lines crossing the mountainside, I guess these also function as fire breaks. Blueberries often grow in these grassy open spaces. I'm told that when the fruit is in season it's worth looking up and down them because you can often spot bears grazing on the abundant harvest.

It's very warm today and I'm sweating out. I haven't really taken enough water with me just because of poor planning. I really wasn't expecting these temperature swings. The climate here is not what I'm used to. It's erratic and alternates between hot and cold, sometimes gaining or dropping several degrees in a day. On one occasion it swung from three to twenty-four degrees Celsius and then the next day it didn't rise far above freezing. I'm more used to a gradual daily creep towards spring and summer, but I guess that's the difference between living on an island and hiking inland on a continent.

All the water I drink, cook and wash with has to come from natural sources on or near the trail, the shelter locations seem to take this into account, often being situated near a spring, creek or some other flowing water. It's not a great idea to drink straight from these, although some people do take that risk. They can harbour unseen bacteria like giardia, carried by beavers, or other parasitic microorganisms. There are different gadgets available to filter water, mine is a Sawyer Squeeze. I have 'dirty' water bags for collection and the device, which is essentially a thick plastic cylinder housing a sealed filtration system, just screws to the top. You invert the bag and let gravity drip the water through the filter and into a clean plastic Smart Water bottle or something similar. If you can't wait that long, you can squeeze the dirty water bag to hurry the process along – hence the name. There are some water sources that are probably best left well alone though, unless you are very certain that you're going to die imminently from dehydration. These include the run off from farm land which contains toxic pesticides, water contaminated by harmful heavy metals, or standing bog water.

Rocky Mountain shelter is down a steep slope and the water source is a further third of a mile down yet another steep slope. I put my tent up in the shelter again but I leave the fly sheet off it this time. Just as I'm thanking God for this beautiful, peaceful landscape a whole troop of noisy hikers start coming towards me down the hill. It looks like a youth group out on a jolly. They're friendly enough, just about every one of them gives me a loud and larger than life "Hello! How ya doin'?!" To my great relief, they walk past the shelter and set up camp in the group tenting area a long way down the hill from me. I can still hear them late into the evening. I'm so exhausted that I decide to split tomorrow's planned thirteen-mile day into a five and an eight, and then I turn in for an early night.

'Early' is a bit of a relative term. They have a phrase on the trail – "Hiker Midnight". Basically, this is bedtime, and it's when the sun goes down. This time of the year that really *is* early, but unless you're not too done in to build a fire, or you want to risk squandering the limited battery life of your head torch, it makes sense to roll with the daylight.

It's so warm tonight that I gradually peel off layers of clothing, what a contrast to the full wardrobe I had on twenty-four hours earlier! Without the fly sheet obscuring the view, I can see the trees through the mesh that makes up the top part of my tent as the sun rises. They look beautiful silhouetted in the early morning sky and just for a few moments I feel peaceful – this is exactly what I signed up for.

The next day is physically hard, starting with a couple of big uphills in the morning. I am definitely not a 'morning person' and typically, I find that the first mile of the day is the worst for me. I think my body protests at being forced out of bed and takes that long to resign itself to the task it's been charged with. I guess it eventually realises there's no chance it's getting out of it and it might just as well acquiesce and get it over with. Once that time has passed, I seem to get a second wind, like I'm primed for the rest of the day and my fat burning metabolism starts to kick in to provide the energy required to see me through.

I stop for lunch at the Caledonia State Park. It's deadly quiet in the park, there's no one here apart from another hiker coming from the direction of the buildings on the other side of the picnic area. He's just passing through but he volunteers information about the important things that we hikers need to know - bins and toilets. There are none open or available. Even the vending machine is switched off. I get out of the rain and sit under a spacious, covered area housing lots of picnic benches and what looks like a large fire place at one end. There's another uphill climb in the afternoon. It's a very sticky and humid day even though it's rained on and off for the whole of it. I even have to strip down to my t-shirt at one point. The path is fairly narrow with rhododendrons pushing in from either side, I wonder how much more difficult it will be to walk through here as the bushes grow and the rest of the undergrowth catches up throughout the advancing springtime.

Later that afternoon I arrive at Disneyland. Quarry Gap shelter has got to be the best kept along the whole of the AT. I can't imagine any others topping this place without actually providing room service. It's maintained by the Potomac Appalachian Trail Club and the sign says that the "Innkeeper" is Jim Stauch. There's a couple of tent platforms, comfy and off the ground. A tiny babbling, yes *babbling*, brook runs through a small rhododendron grove in front of the shelter itself. There's a bear box and a swing seat. The dining area, with an optional tarp windbreak that one can unroll, separates two sleeping areas. The floors of these are painted forest green and the caulking between the logs is painted white. There is even a selection of garden ornaments; dream catchers, a sundial, a couple of plastic frogs, and a castle. There are cut out wooden yellow ducks stuck to the roofed edges of the shelter that I have to walk past and it takes me till the next morning to realise why they are there…as I bend my head (duck) to avoid getting brained. Duh! It's twee and bijou in a sort of surreal "who dumped me on the set of sleeping beauty" sort of way. I keep expecting three little fairies to pop out of the woodwork and start turning things alternately blue and pink. It's beautiful and dreamy and I love it. The slightly underdone ramen noodles I have for my dinner don't even detract from it, come to that, neither does the evil looking spider that I momentarily mistake for a Brown recluse. This place is too nice for anything with necrotic venom to survive here for long... I reckon it'd end up sweet and fluffy by osmosis, turning into some kind of AT version of Jiminy Cricket.

In the evening a bunch of blokes turn up, they've gathered here from various locations in the States to have a meeting about some ministry they're collectively setting up. One guy stops to talk to me and we have a conversation. Not for the last time on my journey I smile at the 'what are the chances?' moment I have. The guy is an intern at the local church in Gettysburg. He'd been humming a song "On wings like eagles" as he walked into camp and we are both surprised when I tell him my trail name. He asks me what I'm really called. He remarks that it's not a name that you hear often these days and he begins to recount a story of someone that he knew when he was on a two-month mission in Hungary who was also called by the same name.

My name is not particularly Hungarian, and I hadn't told him that both my parents are from that country, effectively making my blood, if not my nationality Hungarian. Take it how you will, it's a small thing but *I* think maybe God heard me the other night when I was missing my people and it's His way of saying "I'm right here with you, I've got your back girl".

The next day is very warm, relative to what it's been anyhow, and I drink loads of water. I walk nearly eight miles. The trail has thrown me a bone today; the terrain is very different, it's nowhere near as rocky. I find myself in a pine forest with needles so thick on the ground that it feels like a carpet and the sounds around me take on a dampened and muted feel that reminds me of walking in the snow. Further on, there's a large area where all the trees are burnt, they look like tall, thick, standing sticks of charcoal. The notice board tells me that a controlled burn was conducted here the previous year. I'm grateful for the change in scenery and I'm starting to feel like I might actually be able to do this thing after all.

I pass the marker for last year's halfway point and then a little while later, the original halfway point marker. The AT changes length each year; re-routes sometimes have to be put in place to avoid dangerous rock falls where the trail has eroded, or for maintenance, like the burn area I have just passed.

I meet a lovely local couple that I have come across before, they are a fount of wildlife wisdom and they share some of it with me. They point out tea berries, these grow at ground level in mixed oak and pine forest and are tiny, red, and edible. They also tell me about all the different kinds of snake that are going to be coming out as the weather warms up, and the difference in their behaviours. Apparently, Copperheads are belligerent venomous pit vipers and it's best to give them a wide berth as even throwing rocks at them won't get them to move off the path. Black rat snakes on the other hand are harmless and eat rodents. They also tell me that the last forty miles of Pennsylvania are ankle-turningly rocky. Something to look forward to then...

I tent the night under a dodgy looking tree at Birch Run shelter, but it is still alive so I'm hopeful that it won't kill me whilst I sleep. There's a young girl camping on her own who invites me to share her fire and toast some marshmallows for a bit. We talk and I discover that there is a minimum age limit for solo hiking and camping out in this State, I had no idea. She's seventeen and has just started doing her nursing degree a year early, but for all her young age she's still well versed in forest skills. The little tower she builds from twigs and sticks lights first time and burns well. I'm impressed and I make a mental note of her technique for future reference. It really does come in handy later on. Even though it's windy tonight, the tree doesn't throw any branches at me and I'm still alive in the morning.

An uneventful day sees me walking to the AT museum in Pine Grove Furnace State Park. The place is so quiet, there's no-one around and the museum is all shut up. It's hard to believe that in a couple of months' time it'll be heaving with thru-hikers from Springer trying to swallow copious quantities of frozen dairy product; it's the home of the half-gallon bucket challenge. You're supposed to plough your way through that much ice cream in one sitting. Many actually manage it.

It's going to be minus three tonight so instead of staying at Tom's Run shelter I opt to overnight at the Holiday Inn in Shippensburg...the trouble is that there's absolutely no mobile phone signal so I can't call an Uber and there's hardly any traffic on the road so hitching isn't an option either. There's a lovely young couple in the car park who have just come back from a walk of their own. I ask them if they have any cell service and explain my situation to them. They offer me a ride even though it's nowhere near where they are going, they even have to rearrange the stuff in their car, moving the kiddie's seats into the boot. I'm touched and amazed by their kindness. I'm looking forward to a big burger and a hot shower.

CHAPTER FOUR

The metaphorical 'ultra-lite police' finally catch up with me.

I Uber back to the trail. The walking seems a tiny bit easier to me today although I am still breathing pretty hard when the path climbs uphill. On one of these steep sections, Villain with a 'V' comes walking up from behind me at a much quicker pace than I can manage and it's rather obvious to him that I'm struggling a bit, so he gives me some good advice: never walk faster than you can have a conversation, even if it means that you feel as though you're hardly making any progress at all; it saves your heart working too hard and leaves you with more energy for the end of the day. I take his advice…and then we have a conversation. He started in Springer in January, which is amazing enough in itself considering the appallingly cold weather experienced by the United States earlier this year, but then he tells me about a serious back injury that resulted in several months of hospitalisation and how that's motivated him to travel ultra-lite. And he really *is* travelling ultra-lite. The man's pack looks like he's out for an afternoon stroll and it's hard to believe he's already been on the trail for two months. I am in awe.

His raingear looks like it might actually be waterproof *and* breathable. He tells me what I have begun to suspect – that there's really no such thing and the best you can hope for is that your jacket will be a good wind break. Apparently he's been known to run over exposed balds in the pouring rain in nothing but his underwear and mac, his reasoning being that if he's going to get wet anyway he might as well minimise the number of clothing articles he'll have to swap out for dry ones when he gets to camp. I imagine myself prancing around on top of a mountain in nothing but a sports bra and my knickers, my raincoat flapping around my ears in some mash up of a Gene Kelly and Julie Andrews movie. It's not a pretty image and I decide that the world really isn't ready for that yet.

I ask him about my bear barrel. It's big, heavy and bulky and I've talked myself into keeping it but I think I secretly want someone to talk me out of it and suggest a viable alternative. He tells me that he portions out his food for each day, double bags it in odour proof bags and sleeps with it under his knees at night. In his tent. With him. Not even the thought of becoming bear bait frightens this guy. I am swooning with respect for the man now.

It seems to be a day full of people…well, for the AT at this time of the year at least anyway, and a bit later on there's a couple walking towards me who introduce themselves as Big Red and Peregrine. They've been on the road for a few weeks now and have some good trail information that I'm certain will come in handy later on, so I try and pay attention but I'm not sure that I'm taking any of it in really. All the places they're talking about seem so far from where I am right now and I wonder if I'm going to remember everything they've said. They tell me about a section of the path that's been flooded out by a beaver dam that I'll most likely have to blue blaze around (a side trail or alternative bad weather re-route) and about the rocks at Lehigh Gap which sound a bit treacherous to me. They've managed to find accommodation with various families from local churches when the weather's been really cold just by literally googling places and then ringing them to ask if they can stay on Saturday evenings. They've ended up hosted - shower, laundry and food; all turned out and in a respectable looking state for the Sunday morning services. Nice.

I stay in the James Fry shelter tonight which I end up sharing with a chatty, friendly bloke called Jean. He's from Massachusetts but actually started his hike in Harpers Ferry and is flip-flopping NoBo as well. It's only taken him five days to get to this point. Everyone I meet seems to be travelling faster than me, but his feet *are* pretty mashed up, I guess, from his long mile days. I decide to sleep on one of the bunk platforms tonight, which affords me a bit of extra protection as they're located behind a small return wall bordering the open entrance, but Jean sleeps in the middle of the shelter on the floor in just a twenty-degree Fahrenheit rated sleeping bag.

In the morning he tells me that he wasn't cold. It was minus three Celsius last night! That's about twenty-six degrees Fahrenheit, bearing in mind that the bags are rated for survival and not comfort. My quilt is rated at ten degrees and I was, well, let's just say that if I was a male brass monkey, I'd be short of my reproductive tackle by now. Talk about proper hardcore! It's still cold. The water in my bottle has a thick layer of ice crystals floating at the top, but I am beginning to see the tentative signs of spring starting to show around me. As I pass a shallow pond, I notice that in the centre there are the tiny spikes of water lily leaves just poking up through the surface, making a bid for freedom from the cold, dark water surrounding them, stretching up towards the sunlight above. The new green growth is a welcome sight after days of only bare branches and muddy earth.

I decide that I'm going to try and make it to Boiling Springs today…but my plan doesn't pan out. The trouble is that although I'm following two separate guides, one paper and one electronic, neither of them really tells me exactly what kind of terrain I am going to come across, and of course this has a bearing on how long it takes me to get anywhere. Walking up and down hills takes so much longer if you are constantly doing lots of mini course corrections, zig-zagging from side to side to pick the surest footing. That's a lot of extra steps…potentially extra miles. It's a lot more exhausting too as you have to lift your leg so much higher with each step you take compared to walking on flat ground. I have also noticed that 'Appalachian Trail miles' seem to be suspiciously longer than conventional miles. I reckon that they may well have measured from one geographical point to another one a mile ahead, but without taking into account the extra physical distance associated with the gains and drops in elevation.

There's a labyrinthine rock scramble called "The Maze" to traverse on my route today. Apart from the ambiguous blazes and arrows to negotiate, some of which look as though they have been deliberately painted on to the rocks to confuse the traveller (apparently this has been known to happen when local youth are bored and fancy a laugh, clearly the juvenile delinquents here are of a much more imaginative calibre than back home…), there is also one portion where I have to take off my pack. I throw it up onto a ledge and do an undignified clamber, which I could call a leap just to impress you all…but that would be a lie, and haul myself up after it. By the time I reach the Alec Kennedy shelter I am mentally and physically exhausted and there's no way I'm making it one more step tonight.

I'm quite pleased I've decided to stop in the end because there are a couple of interesting characters here. They have heard of me. Apparently, I am "The Heavy English Lady" and they are not talking about my physique either. Looks like my weighty pack and I have made a name for ourselves and everyone coming from behind seems to know about us. I find this terribly amusing.

Zorro is from Barcelona and gorgeous. He's hiked a lot

of the world's long-distance trails and he regales me with the story of how he got run over by a grizzly bear on the Pacific Crest Trail (PCT). That isn't an exaggeration either, the bear actually ran over the top of him after he accidentally surprised it whilst walking through a thicket of dense brush. He's really, really lucky to have survived an encounter with an armed and hairy steam roller somewhere far north of three hundred pounds in weight, and yet it hasn't put him off hiking. I was awed by Villain with a V but my hero worship has just been ramped up to a whole new level by this guy. He looks at my overweight gear and tells me, "It's all about the hiking and not about the camping". The look on his face suggests that my reputation is pretty accurate and he recommends a few changes I could make to lighten the load a bit.

Feral is a tall, slim, sweet and funny retired serviceman. He's walking the AT and the PCT simultaneously, flipping between the two. When he gets fed up with one, he hops over to the other and picks up where he left off. He shakes his head at me and jokes that my name is too long and my pack is too heavy. Both he and Zorro started their thru-hike in January and, somewhere along the line, ended up walking together. On their advice, I decide to swap out my bear barrel for an Ursack at the next available opportunity. I also shorten my name to O.W.L.E., at least temporarily, until something comes along to inspire me. It never really sits well with me though.

During the night I hear the sound of coyotes howling in the distance.

The next day I walk the final four miles into Boiling Springs that I couldn't face yesterday. There is an ATC office in the town, it's not officially open but there's a lady working inside who comes out briefly to chat. I sign the log book and check out the hiker box which is situated outside the front of the building. Hiker boxes can be found in various locations along the trail, but most often in hostels, and they contain items that hikers passing through have decided to leave behind for whatever reason. For example, you might buy a bottle of shampoo to wash your hair when you're in town but you don't want to carry the extra weight all the way to your next stop in civilization, so you leave it behind in the box and another hiker can then help themselves to it. This one contains mostly ramen noodles but I've seen gloves, waterproofs, sandwich bags, all sorts of things in them really. I also check out the outfitter in town to see if they have anything I could use as a bear bag but they turn out to be mainly geared up with fishing supplies. Boiling springs has a beautiful river that runs through it called Yellow Breeches Creek, which I guess attracts the local anglers.

I make a decision to Uber to a motel in Carlisle with the thought of putting in an internet order. Now that I have decided to ditch my bear barrel, I need to replace it with a viable alternative. Whilst I'm waiting for the order to arrive, I'm thinking I'll do a few days of slack packing. This is when you are based in a hostel or motel for a day or two and walk portions of the trail for a day at a time, taking only the things you'll need for that one day with you, and then returning to your accommodation to sleep.

The bear bag I'm thinking of buying is called an Ursack. There are two kinds. Kevlar ones that are deemed to be bear proof which you can, technically, attach to a tree, or rodent proof ones. These you have to hang from a branch but they do have the added advantage that if you're placing them in a bear box (these specifically designed bear-proof containers are provided at some shelter sites) the mice and rats that can access the container can't chew through your bag and steal, or worse pee, on your food. I order a rodent proof one and I also buy a bear bag hanging kit that has a neat little "rock sock" which attaches to a super strong line. The idea is that you find a suitably sized rock to put in it, shouldn't be a problem around here…there are, like, ten thousand to choose from within spitting distance of wherever you are. The rock gives it the weight needed to make your throw more effective, and I guess the bag might save me from cuts and lacerations when the thing hits me in the head on the way down...leaving me only concussion to contend with. My purchases should arrive in a couple of days' time.

In the morning I get a ride twelve and a half miles up the trail and slack pack back to Boiling Springs south bound (SoBo). It's a lovely day, warm and sunny, and the terrain is as close to normal as it gets; flat with a variety of fields and wooded paths alongside a small river. In some places I get a great view of the mountains that I've been walking along. It's strange to think I was way up there a day or so ago and that I'll be up there again very soon. It's idyllic in comparison to what has gone before. There are patches of delicate little two-tone blue and white flowers growing close to the ground, and some white ones that look a bit like wood anemones. I even see my first chipmunk; it's a lot fluffier than I expected and it has a gingery coloured coat.

I'm walking through an open field and I can see a familiar figure in the distance coming towards me. It's Feral. I really wasn't expecting to see him again as I was convinced that at the speed those guys were doing, they would be well ahead of me by now. He's just as surprised to see me coming towards him and demands to know why I'm walking "the wrong way" in his friendly, jovial manner. I tell him that I've taken his advice to lighten my load, and that I'm waiting for my bear bag to arrive before I can move on up the trail. He seems genuinely pleased at this bit of news. He explains that his dodgy knee has had him off the trail and at the doctor so he's missed a couple of days of walking. There's not much that can be done about it but he's chosen to carry on as best as he can for now, and he's hoping he might be able to catch up to Zorro at some point soon. He also tells me about ramps. Ramps are wild onions that grow in these parts, and when he describes the leaves as short spikey and green, just like chives, I immediately know what he is talking about. I've seen them on the trail and later that day I pick a few to chew on. Feral has been using them to liven up his instant mashed potato, brilliant idea. I've used numerous things to enhance the monotony of my mashed potato too - tuna sachets, chopped salami sticks, cheese, even boiled garlic cloves - anything, *anything*, that will make it not so mashed potato-y, and I'm always on the lookout for fresh ideas. I'm really delighted that I've had the chance to see him again. I hope he manages to keep going.

There's another familiar face further on too, Jean, who's now calling himself Ewey. It's what he used to be called when he was younger and he's adopted it as his trail name. He's sitting on a log eating his lunch and gives me some of his turkey salami. I join him and we tell each other what we've been up to since we last met. A young man, Reader, rocks up and stops too. Further down the trail I will see an entry in a shelter log and discover that it was Zorro who gave him this trail name after noticing that he was always reading the news on his mobile phone. He's a twenty-one-year-old former trail guide who's currently taking a semester off from studying English with Education to SoBo Flip-Flop the trail. He tells me he hopes to become an elementary school teacher one day, he's articulate and intelligent and I reckon that career would suit him well. He offers to do a free shake down of my pack contents, but sadly I'm not staying anywhere near the shelter he intends to stop at tonight so I thank him, but decline. His backpack is the make and model that I would have preferred to purchase if it had been available in England. I'm a bit envious. I bet he doesn't get the same attitude from it that I do from mine. We walk on together for a bit, talking about our experience of the trail so far. His worst moments were being been bitten by a deer tick which, luckily for him, was an adult male as only females and nymphs carry Lyme disease, and having to cross a tricky ridgeline boulder scramble in a blizzard. Wow. I've had it easy up to now.

Just before hitting Boiling Springs at the end of the day, I run into a stocky guy with a big black pack called Turtle coming the other way. As soon as he hears my accent, he says that I must be the "Interesting English lady". That reputation sure has spread! Well, at least I've graduated from "heavy" to "interesting" then...I guess that's an improvement, right? At Boiling Springs, I buy some new insoles for my boots as my Achilles tendonitis is playing up a bit. I've slack packed twelve and a half miles today and marked a significant accomplishment – one hundred miles done.

Back at the motel, I discover that my equipment order has been delayed for a couple of days. I can't stay here and wait that long so I'm going to have to make a contingency plan. The motel is prepared to accept the delivery in my absence and to hang on to it for me. One of the guides I'm using, Guthooks, is on my mobile phone. Amongst other things, it lists services along the trail and is updated regularly. There are contact details listed on here for really helpful people known as "Trail Angels", along with the kind of things that they are prepared to do to help hikers. Some have places you can stay; others offer shuttles between towns. I find one located in the town where I'll be on the day that I need to come back to get my stuff, and I ring her to see if she is willing to do the return trip to pick up my goods. Her name is Mary and she truly is an angel. We arrange where and when to meet up. I breathe a sigh of relief.

I do a small restock in Walmart where I find a cheap poncho for five dollars. I'm thinking it'll cover both me and my backpack and save me getting my raincoat out on warm wet days...and it'll be the perfect accompaniment to my wardrobe if I re-visit the whole dancing in my underwear on a mountain top thing. I also buy some packaging material so that I can send home the things that I no longer need. When I wrap up the parcel, I add a couple of other items that I've bought for my grandchildren's birthdays in a couple of weeks' time, I reason that the extra weight won't push the box over the limit for the price bracket it sits in. The postage is extortionate but I don't want to part with my bear barrel indefinitely so I send it off to England anyway. I pat myself on the back for managing to shave between six and seven pounds off my base weight, which is defined as everything in my pack exclusive of food and water. I spend the rest of the day working on my next YouTube video.

I've purchased a trash compactor bag and use it as a waterproof liner when I re-pack my gear. I move my puffy and quilt to smaller dry bags, ramming them in to make them fit. On advice from Reader, I pack a lot of stuff loose at the bottom to take advantage of those 'fat hamster' gaps. Everything fits better, it feels lighter and more stable and I set off happily on my short, but very steep and narrow, uphill two-mile walk to the Darlington shelter.

Just before I start to ascend, in the woods to the right of me, I see the rusted-out skeleton of a 1950's car lying on what would have been its roof with the remains of its wheels facing skywards. The pistons in the engine are still intact and visible, giving away its age. The front bumper is wrapped around a tree trunk and it's surrounded by reasonably dense woodland on all sides, there isn't a road or even a broad track anywhere near it. I guess it must have crashed and was abandoned all those years ago. I bet there's a story there somewhere. On the way up the hill I stop to talk to a prospective thru-hiker coming down the hill towards me and I encourage her in her future endeavour. Her trail name is Percy, short for Perseverance Pays. A good name, I think.

When I arrive at the shelter site it feels peaceful and relaxing and I decide to stop for the day and take a Nero (nearly a Zero). There's a guy called White Castle here, and he can't quite believe that I have no idea what his name is referring to. In my head I'm picturing tall turrets, drawbridges and knights in shining armour, but it's nothing remotely so romantic or glamorous. He explains that it refers to a popular brand of burger available in the States and that he came by it when he once supplied his namesake to another, ravenously hungry, hiker. Today, he's carrying cans of soda and not burgers. He introduces me to Birch

Beer. It tastes like Root Beer but with an unusual twang in the flavour that I really like. Apparently, it's a Pennsylvania thing. He even takes the empty can away too so that I don't have to pack it out. Quiet Storm, who's camping here in a hammock comes over to join us. She has section hiked quite a bit of the Appalachian Trail already and shows me pictures on her mobile phone of the previous treks that she's done. Both of these two are out on training hikes today.

I end up having a relaxing afternoon just chilling and chatting. They advise me to avoid Cove Mountain shelter, the next one down the trail, as it's quite a long way off the path and not all that great, they say it has a porcupine family living underneath it. I wouldn't mind seeing them, but I don't want to walk miles off the path to stay in a ropey shelter, so I decide that I'll go all the way to Duncannon tomorrow. I take an early night again as I never seem to sleep well in a motel. I'm not sure if it's dehydration from the climate control units or just that I have grown accustomed to being outdoors at night in my tent. That evening, I receive two uplifting emails from a friend, they really encourage me and I fall asleep smiling.

It's an early set off for me in the morning. I want to plod the twelve and a half miles to Duncannon at a slow-ish pace. I make a mental note to remember the advice White Castle and Quiet Storm gave me about the town yesterday – don't stay at The Doyle, they said that in their opinion, it's famous but it's a flea pit with rodents, but to be fair though, they did also say that the food was really good there.

There's a big 'up' along the way and I'm really pleased with myself for getting to the top without stopping, especially as it's humid and hot today. I sweat a ton and wish I'd brought extra water with me. The path is rocky, very rocky. Ankle turning rocks blanket the path for miles and it's very warm and muggy. Just as I am thinking that there is only one more downhill left to go before I get into town, I come to the edge of a cliff. This is Hawk Rock. I can see Duncannon and the Susquehanna river about a mile straight down. The view is spectacular but the only way to get there is down the side of this mountain on these really, really steep rough-hewn rock steps, literally carved into the edge of it. It's the worst thing I've seen so far and I have to swallow back the panic that starts to rise up inside me before it hits the surface and I flip. Once again, I question the wisdom of walking a mountain range when I'm not that keen on heights. I turn my mind to God desperately and try to remember encouraging Bible verses as a distraction technique whilst I descend as best I can, trying to avoid looking at anything other than my feet and where I need to place them next. "You did not give me a spirit of fear but of love, power and a sound mind." Yes, a sound mind, that'd be good round about now. "Be bold, be strong, for the Lord your God is with you". Yes, I'm definitely going to need some balls to get through this one. I am genuinely terrified; I don't know how I do it but I make it to the bottom without having a meltdown but I'm completely exhausted, my legs are jelly and my mind is fried.

In Duncannon I gather myself together sufficiently enough to find a local pizza place and order a huge pizza. This is so impressively massive that it does me for three meals in the end! On the way, a very loud and slightly wobbly looking guy is just leaving a bar on the other side of the street. He shouts across the road at me in barely intelligible words of one syllable, extolling the virtues of The Doyle and encouraging me to get a room there. He introduces himself as a member of staff on his way to work, I think he sounds more like a hammed-up actor and he is quite clearly totally inebriated. I spot The Doyle. It looks like a movie mock-up of a wild west tavern, but it is in fact a bona fide relic from a bygone era. The bar man I met seems like a perfect fit now.

I stay at The Red Carpet Inn a little way out of town instead of risking the rodents...and the crumbling architecture...at The Doyle. They offer a very reasonably priced shuttle service. Result. They are also really nice people and although it's a bit basic, it's cheap, mouse-free, and it doesn't look as though it'll blow over in a breeze. My feet hurt so I promise myself a zero tomorrow to get over the shock of today. I get to thinking that maybe I'm just not cut out for this, there's almost certainly a whole lot worse up ahead and I'm worried I might not be equal to it. I have a thought – maybe things are only frightening when you don't know what to expect because you don't know how to deal with what you don't know. I need to get my confidence back up. I can do this.

The next day I hop into town and resupply properly at the local store. I'm really pleased with the selection of food and how well it packs down. They have a new variety of Snyder's pretzels that I've never seen before – parmesan garlic. Of course, I just have to buy them. They're very tasty but I don't think they'll replace the buffalo hot wing any time soon.

I sit on a bench in the local park to plan the next leg and I realise that I might have to do a couple of longer days, twelve and thirteen miles, and carry extra water with me as the shelter sites are not placed terribly conveniently. The next few days are going to be hard and long but I'll just have to push through them. I have dinner at a diner near the motel. It's mediocre, but to be fair I am still digesting that epic pizza. Hopefully Trail Angel Mary will shuttle me back to pick up my delivery in the morning.

CHAPTER FIVE

Thank God for angels...and motel bathrooms.

I get shuttled into town in the morning and head to the pub in Duncannon where I've arranged to meet Trail Angel Mary. When I round the corner, I see a camper van parked on the side of the road. It's covered with hiking themed bumper stickers and I wonder if it's hers. It is. She's kind-hearted and sweet and I love her immediately. She takes me on the long round trip to collect my package from Carlisle. I write in the log book that she keeps in her van and she takes a photo of me to stick next to my words.

When we get back to Duncannon, she invites me in and I ask her to tell me the story of how she became a trail angel. A few years ago, personal circumstances found her living on the town campground for some time. The place was also used by hikers, and from the stories that they told her about their lives on the trail, it was easy for her to see the effects that long-distance hiking was having on them, so she started to buy them bananas for the potassium. They always tried to make sure that she was ok too. The shared experience of those moments in time has given her a big heart for the hiking community. I learn that she's not been too well recently and that she's got a hospital appointment in a couple of days' time. I am bowled over by her selfless generosity and kindness; despite all her personal problems she still keeps on giving. I see scripture notes open on her desk so I guess it is a pretty safe bet to ask if I can pray for her, she says that I'm the second hiker this week who has done so. Before I leave, she gives me a tip about a stealth campsite that might help break up my journey over the next couple of days. I give her a big hug and I'm on my way.

The path out of Duncannon isn't as bad as the one that brought me here but it's still a bit of an epic uphill for about three miles. This is followed by another mile of ridgetop boulder scrambles, there's just the rocks and nothing else either side but a drop. I get into the zone and realise that if it wasn't for the genuine threat of serious injury and the destabilising, heavy weight on my back, I might actually be having fun. As I settle down to sleep that night, I notice that I've pitched my tent on a load of roots, I hope they don't make a hole in the base. It's going to be a long day tomorrow. I am SO over Pennsylvania and its rocks.

The next day starts out ok. The terrain is loose-rocky with scrambles mixed in. It all just takes *so* long. Eleven point seven miles feel like an eternity, especially as I have to carry water and pitch at an unofficial camp site nowhere near a stream. It's basically a bit of a clearing in the woods with enough rock-less space to put up three or four tents.

A guy rolls in just after I'm done eating dinner. He was worrying that he'd miss the spot and so he's grateful to see me and my bright orange tent. His name is Indie, after Mr. Jones I presume, and the first thing he does is excitedly tell me about a porcupine he's just seen asleep in a tree. I'm envious because it's one of the animals on my wish list. I'm not surprised though as I've seen a lot of partly destroyed trees on my way here with the tell-tale shredded gnawing damage they cause. Porcupine evidence looks a bit like beavers have chewed up a tree, but it's nowhere near water and they don't remove the fallen wood, they just keep on chewing at it and leave what looks like a load of sawdust and wood shavings. Indie demonstrates how to hang a bear bag properly for me; this is just as well because my technique leaves a lot to be desired. It turns out that he tried a thru-hike last year but a bad-tempered rattle snake had other ideas.

My feet hurt a lot and I keep getting bad cramp in the night and it doesn't seem to matter which direction I try to stretch out the effected muscles, it just moves the debilitating pain elsewhere. By the morning I'm cold, thirsty, moody and fed up. I'm up and away by 6am, stopping at the next brook to make breakfast and fill up on water. It's uphill for miles and miles. My energy levels are ok for the first four and then they run out. I'm walking on willpower alone. I can't stop though as I know I'll get chilled to the bone and there'll be no way to warm up again. I decide I really, really don't like being cold.

Nearly thirteen miles later I arrive at Rauche Gap shelter and I pitch my tent on a massive hill composed of re-wilded waste from a long-gone era of iron mining; basically, I'm camped on a big slag heap. The terrain this afternoon was good but the last two miles have killed my feet and knees and now I have a horrible headache too. I'm also pretty convinced that the noise that I've been hearing intermittently for hours now is machine gun fire. Either that or the narrow path that's been winding its way through thick rhododendrons has transported my mind on to the set of a Vietnam War movie. I really need to do less tomorrow.

A local couple are already at the shelter, which is a little way on from the tent site. They're friendly and bring their two dogs over to introduce them to me so that neither they nor I will have a nasty shock if we should chance to bump into each other in the middle of the night. They have tons of food and offer to share. The water here is a proper piped spring. Amazing bonus.

Throughout the night I am entertained by the sound of mortars and helicopter rotors. I later discover that just over the hill and out of sight is a state fire arms depo, and possibly a military base also.

In the morning I notice that one of the dogs is a bit subdued, and on closer inspection it appears that he's got a nose full of porcupine quills. Apparently, he ran up the slope late last night and came back with his nose doing a perfect impression of a pin cushion. His owners leave before I do, they've had to cut their camping trip short so that they can get the poor creature some urgent veterinary treatment. Porcupine quills can continue to work their way deeper into the flesh where they can cause infections if they're not removed as soon as possible, making it an absolute priority to get him some help.

I end up leaving camp later than I customarily do and make up the time further on when I come across the promised beaver dam re-route that Peregrine and Big Red told me about. It takes me just shy of half a mile out of my way but it's a flat stone-less track and an easy quick walk. I'm glad I wasn't tempted to try walking through the chest high, giardia infested swamp the animals have created. I'm told later that they blew up the dam last year but the tenacious creatures re-built it in exactly the same spot again. They put up some kind of notice, but apparently beavers can't read.

Later in the day I come across a river. There's a seriously sketchy fallen tree spanning it, I suppose this represents a bridge? Not fancying my chances on the slippery wood, I opt to wade across, which isn't easy either in the current and on the slick muddy banks. This time, though, I actually stop to swap my boots out for my waterproof camp shoes and zip off the bottom third of my walking trousers in spite of the cold. Miraculously, I make it to the other side without falling in. Just. I stop to have my lunch under a road bridge on the other side and I'm amused that I feel like a proper hobo sitting there on the ground next to my backpack, food in hand.

I camp off the path in the woods again tonight. I've had

to get water from another, wider, river underneath yet another road bridge and carry it all the way up a long and steep slope. The extra weight at the end of the day consumes every last bit of my energy. I pitch my tent in the best of several possible spots, all of which have either small stones or tree roots punctuating them. Just as I finish the heavens open and a long night of torrential rain and thunder begins. I'm stuck inside my tent hoping my money was well spent. Unable to cook, I'm forced to eat dry food for dinner and the rain is so loud that it keeps me awake most of the night. Well, at least I know I can pee in my vestibule if I have to.

I don't drown and I'm stoked that my laughably thin-walled tent has kept me and all my gear bone dry. Result. Everything else is wet though, and my hands end up all wrinkly from dismantling my tent and packing up. It's 'horror movie misty' in the woods this morning and as I walk about fifty yards further up the path, I come across two beautifully flat, stone and root free clearings in the woods. I laugh. Typical. If I hadn't been so done in the day before I would have probably walked this tiny additional distance in search of a better spot than the one that I'd settled on. I plan to walk ten miles today to the 501 shelter. It's close enough to a road that a local pizza place is prepared to make deliveries there.

The ridgeline here is forested and I am surrounded by beautiful bird song as I walk. It's very sunny and I take the time to stop in a clearing and spread my tent out to dry. The dappled sunlight coming through the branches of the trees is just dreamy. I sit and enjoy the gorgeous day, then walking towards me, Indie appears unexpectedly. I thought that he'd be well ahead of me by now but he's had a zero to buy new shoes and visit a relative living nearby. He's only planning on a short walk today so he can break his new footwear in gradually. He doesn't stop for long but continues on his way at a gentle saunter.

Eventually, I walk on to the point where the trail intersects route 645 and I sit down to take the weight off my feet for a bit. Who should I see ambling along the path in my direction? It's Indie again. He's caught up to me, having stopped to have his lunch at one of the shelters on route where he had originally planned to spend the night. The lovely day has persuaded him to rethink his mileage and he tells me he's going on to the 501 shelter, which is just two miles ahead. But by the time I'd got to this point I had changed *my* mind too and I'm not going any further today because my feet really hurt. The insoles I bought in Boiling Springs are just a bit too small on the instep where the boot has expanded from use and there's a ridge. It's tiny but it is enough to have caused a couple of blisters on the soles of my feet. These were small and manageable to begin with but they have now expanded to about three inches long and about two inches wide; one foot has suffered slightly more than the other. I had previously covered the affected area with leukotape, which is designed to act as an extra layer of skin to protect what's underneath. It's so bad that virtually none of the skin on the undersides of my feet is visible anymore there's so much tape. To compound this, one of the blisters erupted suddenly today as I was walking on a particularly rocky bit of path. I felt it go and had to spend a while there and then dealing with it. It's not the sort of thing you can just leave. It's impossible to keep anything clean, so open wounds need to be disinfected and covered up as soon as possible. A foot infection would be a very, very bad thing out here. It is also Saturday, so I decide to get a motel room and see if I can't get to a church service in the morning.

There seem to be more churches in this country than there are people, I'm sure that's a gross exaggeration but there does appear to be one around every corner in all the towns I've been in so far. And the names of all the different denominations baffle me, I have not got a clue what that's all about. Still, I'm curious to see what they're like and I've missed the fellowship.

There's a guy in the car park where I'm sitting who's changing his shoes after coming back from a run. He comes over to me and offers me a lift in a broad Northern Irish accent. He's heard me talking and decided to come and help out a fellow compatriot and he ferries me to where I want to go despite the fact that it's not on his route home and he has to Google the directions as he has no idea where it is. His job in pharmaceuticals has brought him to the States. He's been here for a few months he tells me. I wonder if he finds it comforting to hear the familiar sound of my British voice?

Anxious not to dip out on the pizza I've been looking forward to, I order take out. A large meat pizza with extra black olives. I eat it with gusto…three hours later we are parting company with equal gusto. I've got a bad case of food poisoning. Typical. Weeks of living in the woods, not washing my hands for days on end, preparing and eating my food with those same dirty hands and not so much as a vaguely queasy stomach. I hit civilization and bang, I'm up half the night getting intimately acquainted with the local plumbing. For the first time, I am grateful for the alarming 'suck it all down in one hit' flush action that American toilets have. As someone who has dropped her mobile phone into a toilet on more than one occasion previously, I was perturbed by the certainty that there is absolutely no way you're going to retrieve anything from the pan after you've depressed that handle. When it's gone, it's gone. In a flash. Into the depths of Hades for all I know. On top of everything, I'm shaking and shivering too.

I can't face breakfast. I manage a bland baked potato at a local diner for lunch with a side order of veg, but the moment I see the carrots I know this is not going to be pleasant. I stick my fork in one of them just to confirm my suspicions, and sure enough it is *so* soft that if I so much as sneeze the thing will dematerialise into its constituent atoms. I have experienced their tinned counterparts with more backbone. I *do* drink a root beer though; I'd have to be on death's doorstep to refuse one of those.

I drag myself back to my motel room. Miraculously I

hang on to my lunch but the remainder of the pizza, having made its way through, now wishes to exit rapidly from the other end. Oh joy. I'm alternately too cold and too hot. I collapse into my bed. At least I've managed to book an extra night with reception, and I'm grateful that paracetamol was on my short list when I packed my med kit.

I succeed in eating breakfast the next day, and even walk to the Dollar General and do a bit of a re-supply. I attempt to find some savoury crackers that are actually savoury, but I fail. You wouldn't believe how hard it is to find savoury crackers that don't taste sweet. You have to look so closely at the ingredients on the back of the packet – there's corn syrup in everything here. Everything.

The thought of some foods is still sending my stomach into somersaults and I have separation anxiety when I'm too far from the bathroom, but I'm feeling slightly more human and I'm hungry now. There's a McDonalds close by and I risk parting from my porcelain companion to go grab a Big Mac meal. I truly enjoy it; it was actually nice compared to some of the offerings that have been dished up for me recently. I muse on whether this may well be a contributing factor to the growing obesity problem in this part of the world.

I'm back on the trail tomorrow, but only for three days as I'm stopping off over the Easter weekend to visit the flagship store of an apparently famous outfitter chain, Cabela's, as it's almost directly on my route. I'm thinking of ditching my soft-shell jacket, which I haven't really worn for days now, and my water resistant (hmmn…) waterproof which is just plain irritating in its habit of drenching me from the outside in a storm and from the inside when it's even remotely warm. I plan to replace them both with one coat. My research has turned up a model that proports to be breathable and waterproof. Well, we'll see, but I'm not holding my breath. In any case it'll save me about four hundred and fifty grams. In the meantime, I do another vlog which takes seventy-two minutes to upload. The Wi-Fi here might be free but it definitely can't be described as efficient by any stretch of the imagination.

It has been an exhausting week. The weather hasn't been kind with thunderstorms and even a tornado warning at one point. One did hit, but quite a few miles south of where I am, thankfully. Something I've learnt is that the AT always throws you a curve ball at the end of every day. Just as you're nearing camp and you've started to breathe a sigh of relief, and you're mentally planning exactly what you are going to do to your mashed potato today to make it more palatable, something evil crops up. It's either an epic rock scramble, a river to ford, a steep and slippery knee knackering downhill, or a rock field. Something. Always something. Every. Single. Day. And I live in the eternal optimism that this day will be different, but it never is.

I shuttle back to the trail head in the morning after another attempt at purchasing savoury crackers…failed. But I do find an American version of Lunchables – "Lunchmakers". To my delight they have a mini packet of Nerds alongside the "chips, salsa and cheese". I am ridiculously excited; they are my all-time favourite candy and the thought of having them after my lunch is a real treat. It lifts my mood instantly. Funny how you appreciate the little things so much more when you don't really have anything at all.

I think I'm going to just about manage the two miles to the 501 shelter that I had originally planned to be at three days ago, any further is going to be a stretch after my recent sojourn in digestive hell. In the end I actually manage just over seven and a half miles! It's the quickest I've ever got over food poisoning, forty-eight hours and I'm virtually back to normal again. However, if I don't see a pizza ever again it will still be too soon.

In the afternoon, I come across a very odd bit of forest, all the trees seem to be the same size and they are far smaller than anything I've walked through up until now, about nine or ten feet tall and skinny. It makes me feel as though I'm

Alice in Wonderland and I've drank or eaten something to make me grow. I wonder if they were artificially planted at some point in the recent past. There isn't any sign of potential harvest or coppicing, and they're not standing in particularly straight lines either, so it's all a bit of an anomaly.

Later on in the day, the trail returns to its characteristic rockiness again and I fall over. Well, it is in fact more like a slow uncontrolled roll to the left in three parts - each time I start to tilt I think that I'm going to regain my balance; I regain a few degrees but then continue downwards again. It feels like slow motion but in reality, it's a couple of seconds at most. The thing with a heavy backpack is that once you start to lean in any one direction there comes a point of no return when the momentum just takes you, and even though you think you can recover - you can't, you don't. If you are very lucky, you end up on your back straight away, stuck like a turtle unable to right yourself. If you are unlucky, you end up on your back stuck like a turtle unable to right yourself *after* having banged, bruised and lacerated multiple body parts. I whack my left knee pretty badly but when I examine it later it's mostly ok apart from a deep but small circular gash. It was very rocky today so I guess sooner or later it was bound to happen really, and it could have been a whole lot worse.

When I get to Hertzline campsite there are hardly any viable pitches, the only one is occupied by a local bloke who's chopping up wood with a hatchet. I decide it would be unwise to argue with an armed man so I put my tent up on some rough terrain. It'll do, it's only for one night after all. The man has a lovely young dog with him that he calls River. I resolve to go and introduce myself to him after my dinner. It's chow mein, at least this is the generous description on the packet but it's essentially just fancy ramen. Still, a break from mashed potato is a break from mashed potato – I won't complain.

The man looks pretty harmless, and the gentle way he treats his dog makes me feel confident that he's probably an ok guy. It turns out he's friendly and totally innocuous, his wife has let him out for a few days on good behaviour. He builds a fire and I keep him company for a couple of hours, chatting into the night about our families and about trail gear. He's recovering from a foot injury and recounts a tale of when he fell several feet down the steep slope that descends into Port Clinton in the winter. He says he was so lucky that he rolled and landed on his pack, this broke his fall and saved him from sustaining any serious damage. He also tells me about the bear problem in the next State along, New Jersey, and that in his opinion, it stems from the fact that they have banned shooting bears there. He thinks the answer is to deter them with bullets. I guess in his own way he's telling me that he's packing, and that if we get a furry visitor in the night I won't have to worry as he's got a permanent solution to the problem on hand. He's trying to be reassuring. I think that it's funny how he's just gone to great lengths to tell a single female, travelling alone in the woods, in the most round-about way, that he's armed…with a gun *and* I've already seen his hatchet action. It's probably not crossed his mind that this might just have the opposite effect on most English women. Thankfully I am most certainly not 'most English women'. I feel safe with my food in my tent tonight, I don't even bother to hang a bear bag.

I'm curious to know what species of raptor it is that I keep seeing flying just off the mountainside as I walk. They seem to be ubiquitous and they're big, but not big enough to be eagles. The guy I'm camping with is a seasoned local woodsman so in the morning I ask him about them. He identifies them as turkey vultures. He's walking in the opposite direction to me so we part company after breakfast, and I'm on my way.

CHAPTER SIX
I finally find my name.

I'm walking nine miles today and right from the get go there's a lot of water on the path. I'm essentially walking up and down stream beds. I guess this has been anticipated because, by the looks of it, at some point in the past the maintenance crews have reinforced the trail with crossways wooden logs that stop it eroding, slow down the water, and act as make-shift steps.

The first eight miles are uneventful, as are so many of the miles I've walked on the Appalachian Trail. The majority of the time on the trail is pretty monotonous. You're just putting one foot in front of the other. You would imagine that this gives you the opportunity to think, and to ponder the meaning of life and other grand metaphysical concepts like, you know, why toast always falls on the floor butter side down, and why no one ever talks about how Schrodinger's cat felt about being shut in a potentially lethal box. In reality though, you fall into a kind of 'mind-neutral' stupor. I'm often concentrating on my footing and mentally marking off the time until I reach a landmark, like water, a shelter, a powerline cut, a road…something other than trees and rocks. But I also find myself acutely aware of the presence of God. I feel Him residing in the complex and beautiful natural world around me, in the ebb and flow of life doing its thing, everything in perfect symbiosis with everything else. As I walk, I feel Him around me and within me, and although we're not exchanging words in the form of intelligible language, we are communicating constantly. It's hard to explain. I guess the nearest I can get is to compare it to the experience of being with someone who knows, and is known by you well, *very* well. A close friend, a parent, or maybe even a lover. The depth of that relationship runs *so* deep that it's as though you're sharing the experience as *one* person and not as two individuals in geographical proximity.

I come across an impromptu gathering on a fallen tree by a stream. Marco the German, Achin, and SloPoke all introduce themselves. We exchange a bit of banter but they've been sitting there for a while so they don't stay too long. They're moving a lot faster than me and by the time I get to Eagle Rock shelter they've all set up camp and are sitting around talking. The shelter site is a way off the trail and I have to descend some steep steps, cross a small stream, climb up the other bank and walk along a narrow path before I get there, but the trek is worth the effort as it's a large and comfortable camp site. I sit down with the boys after I've pitched my tent and we chat. They're talking about their trail names.

No one on the AT goes by their real name. I'm not sure how this tradition came about but I guess, apart from being a bit of fun, it's probably a good security measure when you're spending so much time in the company of complete strangers. Most people wait to be given a trail name by another hiker that they meet during their journey. It's usually a reflection on character or a comment on behaviour…so be careful what you do when you think that no one is looking! Of course, you're perfectly at liberty to reject any suggestions that you don't like. To avoid this, and save being tarred with something suspect, some people name themselves before they hit the road. I have been going by the name "On Wings Like Eagles", a nod to the verse in Isaiah that says that "those who trust in God will walk and not feint, run and not grow weary". It's a verse that's had a prominent place in my life for one reason or another for ages now, but it also seemed pretty appropriate given the thing I'm doing. I agreed with Feral that it was "too long" but I don't much like the short version, "O.W.L.E.", either (wrong bird species...), so the conversation they're having draws me in and I listen with interest.

Marco is a big guy with a big pack, he's, I'd guess, in his mid to late thirties. He produces a big packet of Haribo sweets that he puts down on the picnic bench in front of us all to share. For some reason, he reminds me of Marvin, "the paranoid android", from Douglas Adams' Hitchhiker's Guide to the galaxy. He seems a bit melancholic and appears to be stoically accepting his lot as a hiker stuck on the AT. His trail name is unpronounceable and German. I attempt to repeat it after him and give up. When I ask him what it means he replies that its approximate (?) translation is "hiker prostitute". I wonder how he got that one? I don't ask. Achin is a lovely older guy, with a twinkle in his eye and a constant smile dancing on his face. His name is a play on the word 'aching' and the name of his home town which I believe is spelt Aiken. SloPoke acquired his name because he isn't in a hurry. I have a moment of epiphany. That's it – I'm going to call myself "One Speed". I'm determined to walk at one speed, my own speed, some days that's fast, some day's that's slow, but it's mine, no one else's. I don't care who passes me, I'm not running a race here. I'm walking at the speed I was created to be capable of. I'm hiking my own hike. One Speed. They all agree that it's a good fit. We shake hands and I'm officially named.

Later that evening, a friend from my church homegroup sends me a wordless WhatsApp photo of their evening meal. They're having a social tonight and on the menu is…pizza. I laugh out loud, you've got to love that sense of humour! I message back expressing my feigned deep hurt at such a cruel image so soon after my sickening encounter. I'm smiling as I fall asleep. It's been a good day. Tomorrow I should get to Port Clinton.

In the morning I set off on my ten-mile day. I'm looking forward to visiting Cabela's in South Hamburg but I'm not looking forward to the descent into Port Clinton. By all accounts it is very steep and slippery.

I realise that I've been away for one whole month now but it feels like so much longer. I've become accustomed to this life style, it's so simple and yet so hard, the two things are held simultaneously in balance together somehow. There are so few considerations to hold in my mind; I don't have to think about what to wear, there are no appointments or real deadlines to keep, I don't even have to think about how I look, and there's a routine of sorts that keeps me grounded. On the other hand, the things that are left really do matter, they are life threateningly important. Food, water, where you put your feet, what the weather is doing. It's a strange mental place to be living in.

All day I'm anticipating the start of the forewarned epic downhill, and after Duncannon, I just don't know what to expect. Along the way I meet a young couple from Maine, we stop for a while and I mention Cabela's so we talk about gear. The guy does mountain rescue in his home town and has honed his pack down to the absolute essentials. He says that when they go out on a shout, not only does he have to carry his own gear but potentially one end of a stretcher too so it's made him pretty ruthless when deciding what to pack. As I say goodbye to them, another man is walking towards me from behind. He's an older gentleman and calls himself TaDa, like the sound stage entertainers make at the end of an impressive routine. He's training for a Flip-Flop which he plans to start after the festival by the same name that's being held at Harpers Ferry in a couple of weeks' time. He offers to give me a lift from Port Clinton to West Hamburg and Cabela's. His car is parked down another trail that peels off from the AT shortly. He's a local guy so he knows the paths around here intimately and he thinks it'll take him about the same amount of time to get to his vehicle and drive around to the trail head as it will for me to walk there. I tell him I'm slow and that I'm not convinced about this, but he assures me that he is quite happy to wait for a fellow thru-hiker.

I finally come across the fabled steep path and it is just that. Steep. It's mostly dry, dusty, and covered in a layer of loose fallen leaves that hide ankle grabbing roots. There are a few steps, but not enough to help really. For once, I miss the rocks that seem to be ubiquitous just about everywhere else apart from where they'd actually come in handy. I fall on by butt once. It is super skiddy and hell on my knees. It's brick s**ting territory, it would be so easy to get my foot caught up and fall, tumbling arse over apex to the bottom. It wouldn't be so bad if it didn't seem to go on for ages and ages; it's not just a short little slope and, for what feels like a long time, I have no idea how far I am from the bottom. The last twenty yards are made up of horrible steep and deep steps. Not what you want at the end of all that either when your legs are already shaking from the downward strain of having your knees bent almost constantly. But I'm down, and over the road I can see TaDa standing by his car.

It turns out that he's a bit of a seasoned AT thru-hiker. The first time he walked it was in the eighties. We talk about the kit he had to use then, and how heavy the packs and all the equipment used to be. He says that the trail was different then too, in terms of people *and* terrain. One statistic estimates that, since its completion in 1937, well over ninety percent of the whole trail has been relocated, or at least rebuilt. He reckons it's the last time he'll be able to walk the AT as he thinks he's getting on in years now. Clearly this guy loves the Appalachian Trail, even his official number plate reads "TaDa". I ask him how he came about his name and he explains that he's quite a reserved bloke in the real world. The name TaDa somehow gives him the freedom to step out of that and be a more gregarious character when he's hiking. I can understand that, there's a certain kind of freedom to be yourself on the trail that's harder to come by in the 'real world'. He takes me all the way to the doorstep of Cabela's. I wave goodbye and walk through the doors, stopping only to dump my backpack into a trolley.

Well, this store is turning out to be a bit of an experience. The first thing I see as I walk in is an indoor mountain covered in taxidermized native animals, everything from what looks like a weasel to polar bears and all the North American creatures you can imagine in between. Around the corner there's another display, this time of African animals; crocodiles, lions, zebras – the whole lot! No idea what that is all about…they *are* a 'hunting, shooting, fishing' outfitters so maybe that's where the theme comes from. Still, I can't help thinking they'd have been better off using the space for extra merchandise as they don't seem to have some of the stuff I was hoping to buy.

The restaurant on the mezzanine has root beer on tap with free refills. I take full advantage of this and grab some lunch whilst I'm at it. Despite the fact that they don't seem to have any silnylon day packs, I do find a mozzie net for my hat and the exact coat that I'm after. Uncharacteristically, I buy a red one, not normally my colour, but I'm reasoning that it'll double up as a signal flag for my rescuers to spot should the worst happen and I fail to negotiate the SOS button cover on my GPS device. There's a good variety of hiker meals available too and I buy a whole week's worth of dinners. These are a bit pricey but they have actual vegetables and meat in them, real stuff not corn syrup infused preservative laden dehydrated miscellaneous food products. I am SO fed up with mashed potato that the cost of seven days of proper nutrition doesn't even phase me. I'm also discontented with spending too much time and money off the trail. Having to switch out my gear and being sick has resulted in unexpected breaks I did not intend to take. What can you do? I guess I just have to roll with it. It's not going to kill me to sleep in a bed and eat a burger once in a while. At least I've managed to slack pack where I can.

The next day is Good Friday. I find a suitable day pack for just short of eight dollars in, of all places, Walmart. Result. I also notice that there is an *entire* aisle devoted to firearms and bullets here. Unsettling. I can understand guns for sale at Cabela's but the meat in this supermarket is already very dead. What are they going to do? Use the frozen turkeys for target practice? I'm beginning to feel a bit sick and tired of shops now, too many people and too much noise all in one place, and I just want to return to the trail and get going again.

Back at the motel there's a note at reception – Achin is staying at this motel too and wonder's if I fancy meeting up for dinner. By the time I catch up with him he's already eaten but we have a drink together anyway. He strikes me as such a gentle and positively minded man, and it's a pleasure spending time listening to him tell me about his journey. He's brought the remainder of a reel of fluorescent yellow duct tape with him, having used what he needs he offers me the rest. I wind a copious amount around the top of my walking poles, which just happens to be the most convenient way to store it. It comes in handy on more than one occasion before my journey's out. Since I last saw him, he's acquired a nasty rash that extends up his arm in a straight line and is comprised of a series of bubbly looking blisters. He's not sure where he picked it up. Eventually we work out that it's most likely poison ivy and that it was probably the plant's oil transferred from the rope of his bear line that has caused it. He tells me how he lost fifty pounds in weight and trained really hard before coming onto the trail this time. It's made a massive difference to him and he's finding everything so much easier, even the challenging aspects of the terrain, like leaping from rock to rock on the boulders that frequently obstruct the pathway. I'm losing weight myself as the days go on, partly because I'm effectively exercising all day every day, and because I'm unable to carry enough calories to mitigate this. Besides, the last week or so I haven't been that hungry. Apparently, that's quite normal and a phase a lot of hikers go through. So, it's not the repulsive thought of mashed potato having a knock-on effect then? I live in hope that things will become easier for me too as I get lighter. I have a theory that if I can lose enough pounds to offset the weight of my back-pack it will put me into 'negative equity' and my backpack will essentially be carrying me. Not very scientific as theories go, I think it's a subliminal wish to get my own back on my pack after the hassle it's put me through with its bad attitude.

I rearrange my pack yet again and leave behind the items I don't need any more with a note for the housekeeping staff to help themselves or re-distribute the articles and the surplus food that I've left in the fridge. I wish that I wasn't so exhausted all the time and I'm hoping the minerals and vitamins in the hiker meals will help me with this. I resolve to drink more water too as I think that dehydration is also contributing to my ongoing fatigue.

A last trip to Walmart before I'm on my way again. I end up having a random conversation with a local in the car park as I walk towards the store, this seems to happen to me a lot. I think people see the hiker gear and are curious. In the towns I visit everyone either knows someone who has hiked at least some portion of the AT or wants to do it themselves one day. People here are much more open and forward than in England. When I finish at the checkout a bloke comes towards me and he offers to give me a lift to Port Clinton. It turns out that he's recently come back from a thru-hike attempt. He took his ten-year old daughter down to Springer Mountain with him; she was the driving force behind the expedition. His name is Sherpa and his daughter's called Dancing Queen, his wife, Care Package, didn't walk with them, but she took on the role of support crew instead. Everything was going ok until he blew his knee out when he overextended it climbing up a mountainside and had to come home to recover. They're going to give it another go, starting in the middle of the trail this time, after the upcoming Flip-Flop festival in Harpers Ferry.

The trail out of Port Clinton is uphill, no surprises there; the towns are always in the valleys near the water sources. I have no idea what the matter is with me today; I'm panicky and nervous as I gingerly pick my way over the rocks and roots on the narrow path winding its way up the side of the steep hill. It's a hot and humid day. Regardless of how I feel, there is no other choice or direction than forward and, eventually, I start to collect myself together.

I bump into a local guy who tells me all about the full moon walks which take place along this trail, he leads these for his hiking club. I secretly think that this is madness, but I don't tell him that, I don't want to dampen the clearly evident enthusiasm he has for these events. I can barely keep my footing in the broad daylight, how can anyone not be constantly tripping over their own feet never mind the sketchy terrain in the dark? I have to remind myself that these people have grown up here, to them it's their backyard and they have probably been pottering around on these tracks as long as they have been able to walk. For them, it's a different story.

I'm at Windsor Furnace shelter tonight. On my way here I see a spectacular centipede crawling over a log, it's black with orange legs and orange half-moons on the edge of each body segment. I watch it crawling around for a while. Walking down the track to the shelter, I almost step on another bright orange creature, this one looks like a salamander. Later, after a bit of research, I find out that this is an Eastern Newt. At first, I genuinely think it's a child's toy it is so artificially coloured and it reminds me of the small plastic animals that used to come in the hollow Yowie chocolate eggs that you could buy in the shops a couple of decades ago. Then it moves. It's very cute. It makes me smile and I carefully step around it. I spot SloPoke in the shelter when I go to check out the privy. We say hello. I have one of my yummy hiker meals for my dinner. Oh. My. Goodness. It is truly amazing; I savour every single bite. Real food.

The tree frogs are deafening here, it's amazing that such tiny little creatures can make such a racket, I can hardly hear myself think. I know people say that all the time but here it really is true; I can't hear myself think because these tiny amphibians are slowly pushing me into a hypnotic trance. They continue long into the night and the constant repetitive sound drowns out all thoughts in my head, eventually lulling me to sleep.

As I walk back from the privy next morning, I happen to glance down at my feet and there right in front of me is a rock in the shape of a perfect love heart! I laugh out loud as I think about how much I hate the rocks here and the total absurdity of finding one that has taken the shape of what has become a universal symbol for love and affection. On my way out of camp I clock up another milestone – two hundred miles done. I'm amazed that I am still here and that I am still standing.

It's Easter day and I need to walk just over nine miles today. The path's full of rock scrambles for the most part, and I'm quickly drained and exhausted by the mental effort of concentrating and the physical effort of clambering over the boulder fields. There *is* a bit of a highlight in the middle of the nightmarish rocks though – I see a porcupine at last! It saunters across the path in front of me nonchalantly, as though it doesn't have a care in the world…well, not a care about rocks at least. I can't quite believe what I'm seeing and by the time I get my camera out it's waddling off into the brush, but I do manage to get some footage of its cute little behind swinging from side to side.

I pass Pulpit Rock, and walk on to The Pinnacle. It's a big pile of rocks. A really, really big pile. It's a good few feet taller than me and it has a broad base. I reckon it could fill the whole of a decent sized living room to two storeys high. This massive stack has accumulated here over time due to a tradition - every hiker that passes by has to bring a rock with them and add it to the pile. I do just that. At the top of this huge mound is a small stone with a dedication to the memory of a person whose name I can't quite make out. As I'm perched next to the monument on a fallen tree eating my lunch SloPoke rocks up and joins me, we sit for a while. When I set off, I remember a bit of advice Hatchet Man from back at Hertzline campsite gave me about the confusing direction the trail takes just here. It almost doubles back on itself and you have to pay attention so that you don't end up accidentally retracing your footsteps. Thankfully I take the right path. My afternoon walk is a bit of a mixed blessing, it's a nice wide path but it is also all downhill and the constant steep angle with no let-up kills my knees and feet.

Eckville shelter is literally a shed in someone's back yard, there's a flushing loo and a solar shower in a nearby outhouse, and a spigot, which apparently is what they call a water tap around here. The tent site is just across the road in a bit of a garden that is mostly laid to lawn with a path that leads down to the woods. It has tent platforms, one of which I utilize. The first thing I do is block up a suspicious little hole just underneath it with a couple of stones. It looks about the right size for a rodent but I'm not ruling out the possibility that a snake might have had the resident for a snack and moved in. I've done the miles in good time today and I'm early enough to have a couple of hours to just kick back so I have a wander down the path. As I look through the foliage, I spot a flash of colour, it's a cardinal, the first one I've ever seen in real life. It's a surprising shade of bright red. I'm really not expecting this as I equate vivid colours with parrots, and parrots with tropical environments. I guess I've fallen into the trap of expecting things to be just like they are in England solely because this is a predominantly English-speaking country. However, it is a different continent and has a different climate and different habitats, it stands to reason that it will have different wildlife – this includes the birdlife, I guess.

I have a very convincing Chicken Gumbo for dinner and afterwards I potter over to the shelter and chat to the occupants. SloPoke is there and so is a guy called Stripes, after the American flag, I think. He's walking to raise money for a charity and, like so many other people that I meet, has had his fair share of injuries that have kept him from hiking the trail on his original time schedule.

I don't sleep well tonight. I think it's because I had a coffee a bit too late in the day and the temperature rose enough in the evening to make it too hot to be comfortable in my tent. I ditch my sleeping bag liner in the end and sleep under the quilt without it and that seems ok.

Some of my route the next day takes me through state hunting grounds. The lengthy sign 'welcomes' AT hikers…provided they abide by the extensive 'guidelines' detailed immediately below the 'welcome'. I'm pleased that it's not actually the hunting season for anything in particular, and wonder to myself whether they'd quite like to earmark a few days specifically to hunt AT hikers, if the notice is anything to go by. I reckon I'd be alright if they did because I had the forethought to purchase my waterproof backpack cover in a fetching shade of 'don't shoot me' orange.

I set up my tent next to Allentown Hiking Club shelter and gather myself together a bit; there have been a lot of never ending, energy sapping, mentally draining rocks today. I'm tired and haven't coped well with the terrain. In an effort to avoid crumpling up into a messy heap of snot and tears, I engage my brain with wondering whether the fear of rocks is an actual thing and what it's called. Stoneaphobia? Rockaphobia? I look it up – petraphobia, apparently. Sounds about right. I'm so relieved that it's the end of the day and that I don't have to think about anything more for a few hours.

I join SloPoke at the shelter for dinner (Pepper Beef

tonight - yum) and I actually have a proper conversation with him for the first time. He says he brings what he wants with him on his hikes and doesn't particularly worry about the weight. How refreshing. He likes his food and always has some candy on hand. He doesn't have a stove though, so he rehydrates all his meals with cold water, this takes more than twice as long. I'm not sure I could cope with that, one of the things I look forward to after a long and tiring day is a hot meal. It kind of grounds me and makes me feel more human.

I'm not looking forward to tomorrow, these rocks are making me so tired and nervous. Still, in two more sleeps I'll be back in a motel. There's a segment of the trail coming up that has no water for several miles. The only sources are undrinkable due to ground water contamination caused by the residue of a bygone zinc mining industry that lasted eighty years and killed off two thousand acres of vegetation. The pollution was so bad that the trees are only just beginning to grow back again even though it's been a fair few years since they shut the mines in 1980. The whole thing must have had quite an impact on the community. One Uber driver later tells me that the pupils at the school she went to were referred to as the "Zinc Babies" by the other children. This description, although a bit cruel, was in some respects pretty accurate; children from this area were regularly tested and found to be positive for high levels of heavy metals in their bodies. There's no way I can carry several days' worth of water with me. I haven't anywhere to store it and my knees won't cope with that much extra weight. It doesn't seem like there's much choice but to Uber ahead and slack pack a couple of days SoBo from Windgap.

In the night a couple of ATVs turn up at the shelter site and several blokes wearing beige jumpsuits with yellow fluorescent bands get out and start chattering away on their radios. They look a bit official and I wonder what on earth is going on. I also make a mental note that if they managed to drive those vehicles up the trail it will be pretty easy walking for me tomorrow.

I sleep really well and in the morning caretaker Mike turns up, he's complaining about the deep grooves the vehicles have left on the trail and asks me and SloPoke if it was local lads. We reassure him that it wasn't. Based on the description we give him he decides that it was probably the mountain rescue team training a couple of new recruits. It's comforting to know they have a presence in these parts.

My deductions about the way ahead this morning prove correct; the first five miles are a dream…then come the rocks…and the Knife's Edge.

CHAPTER SEVEN
I believe in angels

The Knife's Edge is a rock formation. Imagine a rock stratum that was laid down millennia ago, the boundary between the various layers has been eroded over time leaving a series of flat discs that look a bit like a rough stack of thick American pancakes that are glued together by an imaginary layer of solidified maple syrup or the such like. Now imagine that the whole assemblage has been rotated through ninety degrees, the pancake's edges facing skywards. Imagine this going on for a hundred metres or so. That is essentially the Knife's Edge, an insane sideways sticky up bit of mountain… and I've been dreading it.

Well, the day has arrived and here I am. There's no other choice than to move forward, whatever happens I can't go back. Then I spot this young lad, he can't be more than twenty-one or two, tops. He is literally prancing around on the top of this rock formation like he's some kind of mountain goat. When I pick my jaw back up off the ground, I decide that at least if I fall off there'll be someone to call the mountain rescue guys that are clearly in the area after last night's encounter.

I'm definitely not a mountain goat and I don't fancy my chances of survival on the top of the rocks so I begin to ever so carefully make my way along the pancakes on the left-hand side, trying not to think about the sheer drop behind me. I hear Mr. Goat Man's voice emanating from somewhere above me, he's struck up a conversation and he has the most insanely calm, soothing voice in the whole world ever, it is impossibly serene. He continues to talk, punctuating this, for the most part monologue, with some good tips on where to put my feet and encouraging words at appropriate intervals. My part of the conversation, on the other hand, consists of mostly four-letter words that reflect my state of mind quite clearly. Eventually, I make it across none the worse for wear, apart from my legs, which are now jelly, and my hands, which are a bit sore from gripping the rock face ridiculously tightly. I have the presence of mind to find my manners; I thank him and ask him what his name is. He laughs and says "Mike I suppose, it's a very common name", which I find a bit strange when I think about it later on. Anyway, he stays with me until the terrain gets back to 'normal' rocky for Pennsylvania, even sitting with me whilst I have my lunch, and then he walks on.

He's waiting for me in the car park which is located at the trail head on the other side of the road. The path continues here, up and then downhill to my shelter for the night. He gives me a few directions and mentions that's it's still a bit rocky on the other side of the hill but it'll be ok. I thank him again and I start to climb the hill. At the top I see exactly what he means by "rocky"; it's a boulder fall on the other side. It turns out to look a lot worse than it really is, there is an easy enough way down and at the worst I have to butt scoot down in places but I take it slow and reach Bake Oven Knob shelter well before dark.

I pitch my tent and note that there's no privy here! My eyes scan the undergrowth for a potential spot to dig a hole in the morning, it's pretty overgrown so it won't be easy, but on the up side, no one at the shelter is going to get a flash of my behind. Not long afterwards SloPoke rolls in, he's not a great fan of rock climbing either so I am relieved to see that he's made it over the Knife's Edge in one piece…without a "Mike" to help him through. A German guy turns up a bit later and we all talk whilst we prepare and eat our dinners together. A young couple walk in whilst we're cooking, but they eventually decide to move on, I get the impression that they were after a romantic night out and this place is clearly way too crowded for their amorous intentions.

The forecast tonight is for thunder and it has already started to drizzle a bit. I have to get up in the night to tighten my fly sheet as the temperature has dropped a lot since I pitched it which has caused it to sag and touch the tent wall. I'm not willing to take the risk that it won't leak if there's a torrential downpour. I go over the day in my head. I've almost forgotten that I saw my first black snake today, what with all the trauma. I'm thinking about "Mike". He didn't have a backpack as such, and there was absolutely no one else on the trail today, he seemed to just be there completely randomly and at exactly the right time, and it was miles from the car park. He walked back with me, so it seems as though he didn't have any plans or agenda of his own. What are the chances that a guy with an insanely calm voice just happens to be at the most frightening part of the AT in Pennsylvania at exactly the right time to talk a nervous middle-aged woman over the top of it? It was really strange the way he told me what he was called, like he was making it up off the top of his head or something. All very odd. The man was a saviour. You might call it a coincidence, but I'm pretty convinced that God sent him just for me - goodness knows I had talked to Him enough about the Knife's Edge before I got there! When I eventually return home to England, I have time to think a lot more deeply about today's incident and I am at least half way to convinced that I had an encounter with an actual bona fide angel that day. In any case, I'm amazingly proud of myself for not having a meltdown or bottling it today.

The next day I have seven miles to walk, but who knows what kind of seven miles they will be. I take a selfie with SloPoke as I have a feeling that we might lose touch now that I'm going to do a bit of slack packing over the zinc fields and he's planning on zeroing at Palmerton. I get his email address and promise to send him the link to my YouTube channel so he can keep track of me and have a laugh at my vlogs.

There are, surprise, more rocks today. I guess this State *is* particularly renowned for them. The cheery Uber lady who takes me to Windgap at the end of the day is amazing and lovely. She is so full of life and it's a pleasure chatting to her in the car. Not only does she take me to my destination, she even waits and drops me to a supermarket after I check in to my motel. It's a Giant Food, not exactly an inspiring name for a chain of shops, brings to mind Gulliver's Travels; I'm expecting to find grapes the size of grapefruits and salami sticks the size of telegraph poles. Name notwithstanding, it reminds me of Waitrose and the food is incredibly good quality if a little pricey, I make a mental note to come back and buy a salad from their enormous buffet style self-serve salad bar. I grab some Munchkins in Dunkin Donuts. It's what they're calling the cut out 'holes' from ring doughnuts. Cute. I'm only in here because I've been desperate to visit this iconic US fast food chain since I arrived in the States, and then, after that, I go grab a Burger King meal. Well, I've got to make up that calorie deficit somewhere haven't I? Besides, I'm planning on slack packing fifteen miles tomorrow anyway. When I eventually get back to the motel, I discover that it doesn't have laundry facilities, oh well, at least I can have a shower. I decide that I'd better hand wash my socks and underwear though. When I take off my boots, I'm suddenly aware that my toes feel particularly sore today too.

After breakfast I walk from Windgap towards Blue Mountain Road, my planned pick up point just over fifteen miles south of here, carrying all my water for the day, about four litres of it. Later on, I'm sat on a bit of wood by a dirt track, maybe halfway there, when the German from last night comes sauntering towards me. He stops and we have a conversation. He shares his Werther's Originals, seems like they're a popular brand of candy on the AT, and he tells me all about his trail name, The Wolf. It turns out that his actual name is Wolfgang and all the way through his hike people have assumed that this was his trail name. Eventually a group of lads get to the bottom of it and they tell him that it just won't do; it's considered to be unlucky, so he adopts this shortened version instead. It kind of suits him, he's savvy, tall and humbly self-assured. He warns me that there will be some dodgy rocks towards the end of my day that he's had to climb up and over a few miles previously, they are just before the road I'm planning on pulling off at later today. Oh great, something to look forward to...

The Leroy A. Smith shelter is on my route and I get to it at lunch time so I pull off for a bite to eat and to have a civilized pee. To my delight, I find that some kind soul has stocked the privy with fresh fruit and chocolates. I help myself to the free food as I'm sitting there using the facilities. I can't think of another situation in the whole world where it would be acceptable to store, much less eat, food in a toilet, a dirty, outdoor, non-flushing toilet. I smile at the incongruity.

Further along I have a slightly unsettling encounter with a strange bloke carrying a red jacket, I have no idea why I notice this in particular about him, maybe because it's the same colour as mine? Maybe because it's the colour of blood?? Bit over-dramatic that. He asks me for some directions and says that he's come from an air crash site that he's been to have a look at. I don't really comprehend what he's going on about, the man is rambling without really making any sense. The only bit that I can understand is the offer of a lift, via a beer, as his car is at the road. I'm pretty convinced that he's not in his right mind and probably on something. I'm sure he's harmless but totally off his head. I shake him by making out I'm in a group whose members are waiting for me up ahead. He departs amicably enough and walks off at what seems like an impossibly lightning speed, I wonder how he isn't tripping over all the rocks…maybe he's just tripping?

My feet hurt and they protest loudly as I scramble over the promised rock fall that is today's 'AT end of the day curve ball'. I have another Burger King meal tonight before heading back to the motel.

The following morning the weather isn't great. I Uber back to Palmerton. My plan is to walk north to where I left off yesterday, closing the gap and finishing the polluted water section of the trail. When I get there, it's raining and cold. There is no way I am walking over the rocks at Lehigh Gap, they're the size of cars, very steep, and slick in the wet. A blue blaze winter trail winds up the side of the same mountain, I opt for this instead. This trail is also very steep but a lot safer. I find myself walking in the clouds, they have descended enough to make visibility terrible and the air is saturated. I suddenly laugh; for a brief moment, I have this bizarre vision of all my photos floating around my head in circles – I took out a cloud account to store all my snapshots from the journey and imagine them living in a place just like this…I really need to have a word with myself!

By the end of the day I am soaked through and quite cold. To add to it all, at one point I have to do an undignified and complex one-legged maneuverer to remove a stone that has somehow worked its way into my shoe. It feels like a boulder but it's so small I nearly miss it. It's hard to believe but if I had ignored it there would have been a crippling extra blister added to my collection a few miles down the track. My rain coat is wet on the inside, I'm pretty certain it's sweat from the steep and arduous climb. So much for breathable, Villain with a V was right…but I'm still not tempted to disrobe. Even a day like this has its own beauty. There are intricate and meticulously constructed goblet shaped spider's webs draped between the bare twigs of the surrounding bushes. They provide the 'string' for necklaces of tiny transparent water droplet 'pearls'. Further along there is a small plaque engraved with the names and date commemorating a wedding on this exact spot less than a year ago. The inscription invites passers-by to add to the little piles of rocks carefully balanced one on top of another. These impromptu structures are known as "rock people". I guess not everybody hates Pennsylvania's rocks as much as I do.

I end up having to wait twenty minutes for an Uber to get me back to Windgap and by the time it arrives I'm shivering and properly cold. Nevertheless, I decide that three Burger Kings in a row is probably a recipe for a heart attack in a recyclable cardboard container, and so I pay fifteen dollars for the most epic salad ever from the Giant Food to mitigate the effect of all that grease. It is SO yummy!!!

My knees, ankle and feet are really, really killing me today and I just want to stop and take care of them but I also need to push on and get through Pennsylvania and its never-ending rocks. I can see where this State's nickname, "Rocksylvania", comes from quite clearly now. It's not just the physical aspect of the rocks I hate, they seem to be doing a number on my head too.

As I lay in bed before I drift off to sleep that night, I wonder what it is *exactly* that I find so hard to cope with. I realise that the rocks are making me feel claustrophobic, they give me the illusion that I'm trapped, that I'm stuck with no way forward or back. Day in, day out, all I see is those rocks; I have no way of knowing what is ahead and whether I'll be able to handle what's coming when I'm barely holding it together now. They make me feel properly panicky when I realise that there is no quick escape route. No exit. No escape. Trapped. It reminds me of a horror movie I watched once where all the routes out of this particular village just led back into the same village – there was no way out. Obviously, it must have made a bit of an impression on me. I remember another time that I had a similar feeling when I first started my supermarket food delivery job. I'd dropped off some shopping and I just couldn't find my way out of the rural village I was in, somehow the Satnav kept taking me round in loops. I had a hard time swallowing back the rising panic but thankfully I got out of there eventually. It seems ridiculously funny looking back on it now, more like a comedy than a horror. I do hope New Jersey is different, by all accounts it is. I've been told that, about a dozen or so miles in, the rocks diminish.

The following day it's a bit windy and the tall skinny trees in the grove I walk through in the morning sway alarmingly. I recollect the afternoon walks my parents used to take me on in the Surrey Hills when I was just about old enough to negotiate a flat woodland path without a buggy. I remember the noise the trees made in the wind, it seemed so loud to me then, and when they moved it always felt as though they would just carry on bending until they fell to the ground around me.

My ten miles take me past Wolf Rock. I've been warned about this, and as my left knee is causing me a lot of pain today and feels like it's threatening to pop, I'm contemplating blue blazing around the base of it on the wet weather trail. As I approach the point where the paths divide, there's a slightly frazzled looking woman coming towards me. I ask her what Wolf Rock is like today in this cold, damp weather and I explain my plan to possibly take the bypass. Her response is a very emphatic "Take it!!". I want to laugh at the super serious expression on her face which says she *so* wishes she had taken it herself. I don't need telling twice, I blue blaze it. Just as well I think, because even with this slightly more manageable option my right foot is doing something funny by the time I get into camp. It almost feels as though the arch has completely collapsed, with every step I take it's as though the tendon that runs the length of my foot is bottoming out and hitting the ground, it feels pretty agonizing. I'm almost too frightened to take my boot off to investigate. When I eventually do, I find it's nothing quite so sinister. It just looks as though I've badly bruised it, probably from an impact with a sharp rock; my boots are suffering and they're no longer offering the protection they did a few weeks ago.

Tonight's shelter has the water source listed as a spigot in the back-yard of a retreat centre that's a little way down a track. Guthooks guide mentions that this is switched on seasonally, and I'm concerned that I'm here a bit too early. Sure enough, the thing is off. I have a conversation with a guest who has just arrived for a few days retreat. I explain my predicament and he really kindly takes my dirty water bottles off me and fills them up from the tap inside the centre. He even brings me out a can of Seltzer. What a nice guy.

Again and again on this trail I have encountered good people who are willing to help, often offering assistance before I even have to ask. It makes me feel humbled enough to want to cry from the overwhelming emotion that wells up as a result of their selflessness. I am so grateful. It's hard to put into words how much of a difference even little acts of kindness have made.

It's an interesting night. A scout troop turn up. They decide to tent on the other side of the track that runs through the shelter area. They were also hoping the spigot was turned on as several of the lads have blown through their water rations during the day and left themselves dangerously short. Their leader was contemplating Ubering to the nearest shop to restock their supply. I tell him about the guy who helped me out earlier and he decides to go and knock on the door of the retreat centre instead. For the most part the kids keep the noise down during the evening. I'm not looking forward to the state of the privy in the morning after twenty young boys have been through it though…maybe I'll just dig a hole.

Not far from where my tent is pitched is a mobile phone mast in a clearing, there's some weird banging noises coming from it in the night, I'm pretty certain that it isn't the scouts, and when I shine my red torchlight in that direction, it stops. Like something has seen me. I decide that I'm better off peeing in the vestibule tonight than tangling with whatever four-legged creature happens to be lurking this close to human habitation, it's clearly not frightened of people.

I strap up my knee the best I can and resolve to get some KT tape and a knee brace when I get to Delaware Water Gap, which should be tomorrow. They say necessity is the mother of invention and I've kind of proved that right; my current handicap has caused me to learn a new skill, one that I thought would be just about impossible for a woman to successfully master. I can pee standing up! Oh yes, it is entirely possible. Who would have thought? Have you ever tried getting up from a squatting position with a busted knee? Not going to happen. It won't support your body weight and you'll have to claw your way up using a tree or push your way up on your poles...which have probably fallen into the potentially poison ivy laden undergrowth by the time you've finished. Want to know how it's done? Find a tree, put one hand behind your back to lean on it and the other one holds your trousers out of the way. Ok, so you do have to bend your knees slightly and lean forward so your bottom's hovering between the trunk behind and your feet in front (the angle of the lean determines your aim, you could probably write an equation if you were so inclined), but to all intents and purposes it *is* still standing. I took a bit of a risk discovering whether this was doable...especially considering the distance between me and the nearest laundry facilities...but when you have no choice, you have no choice, and it makes you a whole lot braver.

I'm really feeling low, not just because of the physical pain and the rocks, but because I seem to be living in dread of what's coming up next and whether my anatomy will cope with it. Pennsylvania has done a number on my head and I'm seriously wondering if I'm cut out for this and whether I can even make it to Maine by mid-July, which has to happen if I'm going to manage a thru-hike this year. I lie in bed and re-evaluate what it is that I am doing here. I know that I can't keep putting the pressure on myself to do long miles. I take a mental step back and look at it from an outside position. My knee and ankle are going to blow out unless I reign in the miles for a few weeks, there's a whole heap load of difference between what I could manage on flat terrain at home and this, especially considering the ongoing issues uphill with my Achilles and downhill with my knee. If I keep on like this I will be out of the game in, I reckon at most, a couple of weeks in any case. I try to be positive and ask myself what it is that I am actually enjoying about this experience. I guess the answer is twofold: I love living outdoors, it's liberating; I love stopping to talk to people I meet, it's invigorating. I decide I have to make these two things the priority and forget about how far I can get, forget about a thru-hike and just enjoy the ride. I suppose I kind of knew this was coming when I took the name "One Speed".

I'm still feeling pretty fragile when I wake up. It's cold and wet and rocky. I feel like crying but I refuse to have a melt-down. I'm focussing all my attention on getting out of this State. Later today I will be in Delaware Water Gap, from there New Jersey is just across the bridge. Not long now. I need to cross that State line for the sake of my sanity.

CHAPTER EIGHT

Yellow bottomed bumblebees make me cry

Delaware Water Gap is a lovely little town, I like it as soon as I walk into it. I give myself enough time here to get my laundry done as it's been ten days since I had the opportunity to wash my clothes, and to pick up the medical supplies I need to keep the various bits of my body going that are threatening to give up in protest. It's still very cold, often dropping to just below freezing at night. I hear they've even had unseasonal snow in Chicago this year. I hole myself up in a delightful little pie shop, the Village Farmer Apple Pie Bakery. It reminds me so much of a place near my home where I used to take my grandchildren sometimes. The counters are filled with an array of yummy food, both sweet and savoury pies of every flavour you could possibly think of, and the coffee's pretty good too. I choose a large slice of the most flavoursome lemon meringue pie I have ever tasted, and I savour each bite slowly and carefully. Heaven. It's nice to feel a bit normal and forget about the rocks and my knee for a while. There's an outfitter in town and I stock up on hiker meals. I also buy a pair of Dirty Girl gaiters, there are so many colours and designs to choose from. I settle on some green camo ones just because they match my hat. They're not cheap but they will stop all the little fragments of gravelly stone and stray bits of undergrowth from working their way into my boots. Talking of which, they've been put through a lot by the Pennsylvanian rocks and they've started to disintegrate a bit so I consider swapping them out, but the store doesn't have anything suitable and I reckon they might just, hopefully, make it through another hundred miles or so.

I make a late start in the morning, stopping for an early lunch at the pie shop to top up on calories before I set off. As I walk past the houses on the way to the bridge that crosses the Delaware river, I glance over and see that someone has painted Oscar the Grouch from Sesame Street on their metal trash can, it's just like the one he lived in on the series. I smile. It isn't raining, I'm not cold, and the sun is shining. It's shaping up to be a good day and my mood is buoyant. As I make my way over the bridge, I can see something brightly coloured painted on the path ahead of me. It's the State line! I cannot believe I have actually survived what is considered to be one of the most gruelling States on the trail. All two hundred and twenty-nine miles of it. I stop and inhale deeply. It's an emotional moment, I can't quite describe how I feel. I think it's a mixture of relief and euphoria. I am under no illusion that geography is no respecter of manmade territorial boundaries, so I know that the rocks won't immediately disappear when I step off the bridge, but the landmark below my feet is a major milestone, and mentally it's very important. I feel somehow lighter and my sanity tentatively creeps out of hiding.

I'm walking slowly to make the most of the lightness in my spirit and the beautiful day. There are a few rocks, but the whole landscape seems to have somehow changed. The trees are a bit different and the woods I'm walking through are more interesting and prettier, greener maybe. I'm liking New Jersey so far. The fact that I have to collect water from a stream that's about half a mile off the trail and carry it up a reasonably rocky one-and-a-half-mile incline into camp doesn't alter my happy mood. On the way I meet a guy called Popeye. He tells the story of how his thru-hike last year was curtailed by a severe injury that he sustained when he slipped on a wet wooden bridge in New Hampshire. He hit his back on one of the rocks anchoring the structure in place and fractured two vertebrae and his pelvis. There was no other choice than to walk the twenty miles out of there before he could find help. By the time he did, he was in agony and realised just how bad the damage must have been. I guess he was running on adrenaline. He describes the White's in New Hampshire as "a vertical rock fall" that can no way ever be remotely described as an actual trail. My knees and feet are not up for that. I have nothing to prove and I'm glad that I have decided that enjoying the journey is paramount to me. I guess I'd like to walk the southern portion of the AT, but for now New Hampshire and Maine can keep to themselves.

I'm beginning to realise that I have seriously underestimated the difficulty of this whole expedition. I had no idea how frighteningly difficult it would be; this terrain is so far away from any reference point I've ever had. I guess the closest I've come is on a visit with some good friends of mine in Yorkshire. They took me to a place called How Stean Gorge. There's a narrow rocky ledge that runs either side of a river that has chiselled its way deep down through the rock to form a limestone ravine about half a mile long and around eighty metres deep in places. The portion we walked was specifically set up for unskilled visitors, had hand rails in the worst segments, and they made us wear hard hats. I was still petrified and I seem to remember I swore a lot! It makes me laugh when I think of how scared I was then in comparison with what I have done here so far. I wouldn't even have said that some of what I have walked lately qualifies as an actual trail at all…more like an accident waiting to happen. And amazingly, none of my research turned up any of this. No one talks about these elephants in the room. The hikers in America must be a hardy bunch and clearly take all these things in their stride – quite literally.

The Backpacker Campground is large and spacious, there are plenty of good sites to choose from and it's fairly open. It even has two bear boxes. I pitch my tent and I have the whole afternoon to myself. When I embarked on this adventure, I imagined that I would have lots of time to sit and contemplate, to reflect on my life and to think about the future. So far, I haven't managed that for more than ten minutes at a time. The uneven path commands my attention for virtually the whole day, and all the other tasks like finding water and setting up camp take up the remainder. By the end of each day I'm so tired that I go to bed and just fall asleep. If I have the opportunity to talk to people, I make that a priority as I spend so much of my time on my own that I need the companionship of others to regenerate. The trail can be quite a lonely place and I might not meet a soul for miles. I don't particularly enjoy being alone, that said, I do need to be in my own company sometimes otherwise my head would explode. I guess I'm a strange mixture of extrovert and introvert all rolled into one. Today I have the time, energy and opportunity to stop and think.

I walk to the edge of the campsite, it's the furthest point from the trail and there is a beautiful view which, for once, is not a sheer drop but a sparsely wooded slope with lots of blueberry bushes. They are in flower and a number of cute little yellow bottomed bumblebees are collecting nectar. I see a tiny seedling that has somehow found a way to germinate and survive in the rotten hollow of a fallen branch, a splash of green in a sea of brown. I wonder at the tenacity of life. Just up from where I'm standing is a decked wooden area, the notice says it's the camp caretaker's platform. No one is occupying it today so I walk over there and sit down with my legs swinging over the edge. For a while I just watch the flowers and those delightful little bees. Gradually I begin to relax. It's so beautiful and quiet, there's no one around and eventually I just begin to cry. I don't even know why really, I guess so much has happened in the last few years – it's as though I've somehow been holding my breath and I have found a safe place to exhale.

I sit there for the rest of the day, alternately smiling and crying as I chat to God about all the things that I've fought my way through over the last half a century, it sounds like such a long time when you describe fifty years like that. I'm weary and worn. Amongst other things, two failed marriages, life as a single parent with all the financial and emotional challenges that brings, and the slow death of my father from leukaemia have each extracted a toll from the bank of my internal resources which I have neglected to repay. But on the flip side of that coin is a richness and abundance that comes from experiencing all those things. It's made me laugh harder, to see beauty more often, to shun the superficial, to dig down deep for the positive, to value truth, and to try and accept others right where they're at, no judgement. And through it all God has been my friend and companion, he sees me - all the way through to the core of me, absolutely all of me…even the bad bits that aren't for public consumption. And I know he still loves me, just as I am, like a good dad who longs for his beautiful daughter to have the best, to be the best, and gently encourages her to become all that she can be, patiently and kindly. No secrets, just trust. I wouldn't change one minute of the past; it has grown me into the woman I am today. I'm not perfect or polished, but I'm me and that's good enough, and I am 'enough'. Who would have thought those dear little fluffy yellow bottomed bumblebees could bring out so much emotion?

Soon after leaving camp in the morning I walk along the bank of Sunfish Pond. In places the water encroaches on to the path, which is made up of large uneven rocks. It's very foggy and the far shore is shrouded in mist, the water is perfectly still and it's perfectly quiet, it feels surreal and otherworldly. I imagine that the river Styx, the passage between the land of the living and the world beyond death in Greek mythology, might have looked just like this. Any minute now, I expect a skeletal, black cloaked figure to appear rowing across the water towards me accompanied by Chris De Burgh singing "Don't pay the ferryman" in the background. A metal tablet embedded in a rock informs me that the pond has been a "registered natural landmark" since 1970 and "possesses exceptional value in illustrating the natural beauty of the United States". I would have to absolutely agree with that statement. It is truly captivating. Later I pass Catfish Fire Tower, the metalwork and sides have been painted a rusty red colour which stands out against the backdrop of a moody grey clouded sky.

As I'm walking along the path, I realise that I am genuinely exhausted. I remember that recently someone, I can't recall who, said to me that the trail has a way of chewing you up and spitting you out. Today I'm thinking, "Ain't that the truth!" I camp that night in a clearing in the woods, I don't think you could even describe it as an unofficial campsite, but I've walked far enough today.

In the morning I'm cold. The first part of the day is ok but then there are more rocks and I'm freaked out by a mini rock climb; I stow my poles and make my way to the top. It's not all that high, or that difficult, but I think my current state of mind has caused my mini meltdown. It's not helped by the fact that the pain in my knee and ankle is an ever-present companion on the periphery of my senses. There's a lot of ridge walking later and I find myself on the edge of despair – they lied about New Jersey, there absolutely, definitely *are* rocks. A lot of rocks. It reminds me of a song from the movie Fievel Goes West. One line of the lyrics goes something like this: "There are no cats in America" ...but there were... and I'm humming the tune to my own cynical version – "There are no rocks in New Je-er-sey". I resign myself to the fact that the trail is just like this and that's it. There will always be rocks, just like there will always be a curve ball at the end of the day to sap the last remaining vestiges of my energy. My optimism and positivity are slowly evaporating and my mood is slipping downhill.

There is a brief respite when I meet a guy called Beach Bum. He's got a ten-year plan to walk the AT, he picks a chunk to complete each year. I can see exactly why this would be a great idea and, if I lived in the States, I think I might have decided this was a good strategy for me too. Sadly, I don't and my options are a bit more limited. I meet him again when I stop at Brink Road shelter for the night.

I wake up still a little emotional and still mentally tired. Today is my grandson's birthday, he's seven. I make a note of the time difference between me and the UK and resolve to WhatsApp video call him later in the day, cell service allowing.

I need to resupply today and there's a deli-style mini supermarket just a small distance off my route this afternoon. There seem to be a few of these at various points not far from the AT. Typically, they have basic goods including your predictable hiker supplies like mashed potato, oatmeal and tuna sachets, but they also have a hot and cold food counter with things like cooked chicken and salads. Some even do burgers and pizzas. Wherever I can, I try to take advantage of them and buy at least my lunch there; it gives me a hot meal that I don't have to use up any of my gas to produce, and a bit of interest and variety in my diet too. The smells coming from the counter at the one I visit today literally make my mouth salivate. I'm surprised I don't have to ask for a mop and bucket to clear up the puddle of drool I'm sure I must be producing as I stand transfixed, staring at the huge variety of home cooked food on offer. What shall I choose? I want to eat it all! One of the local lads in the queue behind me must have spotted my dilemma as he suddenly pipes up with a recommendation, pointing at an amazing pile of spicy chicken, apparently it's his favourite and it's never disappointed him yet, so I run with it and order probably more than I can physically accommodate in my belly. I compliment it with a side of thick cut, fresh coleslaw. As predicted, I'm unable to eat all of it and have to bin the leftovers as I can't afford the space the packaging will take up.

Later that day I pass Culver Fire Tower. It marks my three hundredth mile on the Appalachian Trail. I'm still here and I'm still moving, at one speed, one step at a time, but forward is still forward. I don't want to quit.

When I arrive at Gren Anderson shelter, I eat the supplies that were originally budgeted for today's lunch. I sit on the edge of the shelter platform before I turn in for the night and think about my day. I'm glad I managed to get through to England on my phone and I'm thankful for the hot meal I had in the middle of the day. I walked seven miles today, tomorrow is going to be a challenging thirteen, but that's tomorrow. Today was good and my metaphoric glass is just over half full. I call that a win and head off to bed.

The next day starts off with a wet pack up and continues to be damp and foggy. Visibility is limited and I'm pushing just a bit too hard today and it's making me careless, consequently I slip over twice on slick rocks. I think I may have damaged my right knee as a result and it's playing up as much as my left one, so is my ongoing Achilles tendonitis which has gravitated to the insertion point on my heel now as well. I'm physically done in. There have been some particularly difficult rocky ascents on my way to Highpoint shelter including Sunrise Mountain, one of the Highest mountain peaks in this State. A large covered but open structure held up by substantial rock brick pillars and a similarly constructed mini obelisk are the only things to be seen today as the view is entirely obscured by cloud.

I'm relieved that I have arrived in one piece, mostly. It hasn't been a totally awful day though, all through it I have had the company of eastern newts. I must have seen dozens and dozens of them in the undergrowth around me and even on the path. I have been extra careful to avoid squishing them by accident. I notice that they have often been in twos and wonder if it might be the mating season for these tiny, bright orange amphibians. They added an unexpected cheery colour to the murky day and the way they move in a funny little wiggle makes me smile, without fail, every single time I see one. Today, that was a lot of smiling. I think they must like the damp atmosphere created by the fog and mist hanging in the air so close to the ground.

I encounter a new type of terrain the following day, I'm basically walking through swamp and bog. In places, some kind souls have built single track walkways out of planks that are anchored into the ground and are for the most part sturdy. In places though, they have rotted and tilt dangerously, or unexpectedly lift if I don't place my weight directly over a support, threatening to dump me in the foul smelling, shallow muddy water. Once or twice I have no other choice than to wade through the mire, side stepping great big clumps of what I think might be skunk cabbage that obscures the ground below making it impossible to gauge the depth of the squelchy mud underneath.

I have had a few bad days, very bad days. I'm beyond exhausted. I am physically and mentally in pain and I am well and truly sick of eating the same old dehydrated food. I have even got to the point where I cannot actually swallow oatmeal any more, no matter how hungry I am I can't get the stuff to go beyond my mouth. How is that even possible? I love food and I am not a fussy eater, my figure is testament to that, so how can it possibly be that my swallow reflex just doesn't work when I try and ingest even a tiny spork full of any oatmeal-based breakfast cereal? I've tried putting granola, Nutella and even coffee in it. It's no good. It won't go down. It sounds amusing, and to be fair, at any other time I'd probably laugh about the absurdity of it but when food becomes a problem, I know I'm really in trouble. This trail is well and truly 'whipping my ass'.

It's mid-morning and I'm feeling pretty miserable as I drag myself along. I'm desperately talking to God, asking Him to do something, anything, to break this funk I've fallen into. I just need…I don't even know what I need. I just know that I am definitely not ok and I need to not be not ok.

CHAPTER NINE

Sola Deo and apple cider doughnuts fuel the 'Stairway to Heaven'.

Unexpectedly, I spot a flock of Scarlet tanagers. The vibrant red of their plumage cuts through the green leaves of the trees where they're perched and I stop briefly to take a few photos. As I walk on, a young family appears from around a bend in the trail up ahead. We stop to talk to each other and they offer me a couple of oranges which I cheerfully take; fresh fruit is a luxury I can't afford to carry as it's mostly water, and water weighs a lot, so this is a real treat. They introduce themselves as Banzai, Hot Drinks and Maplecakes. Banzai begins to tell me that he's the pastor of the Presbyterian Church in Unionville, a small town just over the State line in New York and about five minutes' walk from where we're standing. He barely has time to mention that they run Sola Appalachian Christian Retreat, a ministry that supports hikers, before I stop him in his tracks and tell him that they are, quite literally, a Godsend. I get very emotional, and it's about all I can do not to dissolve into tears. They invite me to stay at their house tonight and accompany them to church the following morning, and I gladly accept. As we walk back into town, they tell me that they've only just moved up from North Carolina three weeks ago to be in a trail town where they can offer passing hikers some hospitality and respite on their travels. They were checking out the local trails and had decided at the very last minute to take a turning that they don't normally walk down which brought them onto my path. If I hadn't stopped to take a photo of those brightly coloured birds, or if they had chosen to walk their usual route, we would have missed each other completely. What are the chances? It turns out that I am their first guest too!

There's a massive double blow up mattress already set up as they've just said goodbye to a relative who's been staying with them. I have a whole room to myself and I can shower and do laundry without having to run the gauntlet of a motel corridor. They are kind and welcoming and I feel like I'm accepted into the family immediately. It is *so* good to be able to just relax and talk about how I'm feeling and where I'm at emotionally and spiritually. I can almost physically feel the stress sliding off my shoulders. Banzai completed his AT thru-hike a few years back so he can relate to my situation. He introduces me to the concept of type two fun. Type one fun is when you are actually having fun – going out for a coffee with your friends, eating the best pizza ever (…well, maybe not that…bad example…still too soon I feel…), or watching a really good movie, you know - the kind of thing that makes you feel alive and warm inside. Type two fun is miserable, often terrifying, and makes you ask yourself why you ever thought it was a good idea whilst you're actually in the middle of it. However, later, when it's over and you're recounting the tale to other people, it makes you smile; you become animated with enthusiasm as you recall every small detail and remember how unquantifiably awesome it was…and that's when you experience the fun. A bit like a delayed emotional response now the danger has passed, I guess. Simply put: the fun is in the telling, but it scares you to death at the time. I realise that I am having a whole heap load of type two fun on this trip and now I'm looking forward to looking back on it.

I meander into town and stop to read the parish bulletin board. There's a poster headed "Bear Notice". Apparently, one has been seen wondering up and down the high street and has managed to help itself to the townsfolk's garbage. I know it's not really funny but I laugh out loud anyway, I wonder if he got away with a pic-a-nic basket or two? I reckon this four-legged dumpster diver was probably smarter than your average bear, Yogi would be proud. I can smell some wonderful aromas coming from across the road. The sign says "Annabel's Pizza", and against my better judgement I cross over to have a look through the window. They have some unusual varieties of awesome looking pizzas displayed behind the counter. I decide I'm hungry enough to risk it and order one labelled "Caesar salad". It's delicious. Looks like I'm over my pizza embargo then, that took about a decade less than I thought it would. Starvation clearly does funny things to your appetite! I find the local deli and do a resupply shop for the next few days.

By the time I return, there's another hiker there called Uncle Gramps and a bit later he invites his friend Home-school to come and join us as well. We all do our little bit to help get the dinner ready and there's much conversation long into the evening. As I'm falling asleep, I thank God for looking out for me; just exactly what I needed, just exactly when I needed it. I'm still not sure how I feel about the trail, but I do know that my mood has picked up since this morning and I have definitely been lifted out of the rut that I've been wearing a deep groove into over the last few days. I feel that at least I have the breathing space to evaluate my circumstances and give my battered body a bit of a break.

The next day we all walk over the road to the church. There's a Bible study meeting in the hall at the back of the building with breakfast laid on. I enjoy listening to the thoughts and ideas people are sharing and contribute some of my own; it's good to get my brain working on something other than path navigation. After the service itself, there's a 'pot luck' lunch. Today is Cinco de Mayo, a celebration that originally commemorated Mexican victory as underdogs over the French at the battle of Pueblo, but these days it's been adopted by the Americans. Most of the food brought by the guests to share has a Mexican theme. There are so many exciting tastes, loads of variety and it's heaven for my flavour starved pallet. I don't exaggerate when I say that there isn't a dish I don't enjoy, it's like they pulled out all the stops and brought the best, and the company makes it even more enjoyable. Good food, good conversation.

I spend the remainder of the afternoon working on my next vlog and just chilling out. We sit and talk again in the evening. I explain to them that I'm not sure if I can carry on because my body and, to a certain extent my mind also, just feel broken. Uncle Gramps and Home-school tell me that in their experience, at some point or another every hiker hits a wall, often more than one wall, and that it's quite normal to get to the point where you feel totally exhausted emotionally and physically. These two guys have both been out on the trail a lot longer than I have, so their wisdom reassures me. I genuinely feel better knowing that it's going to pass if I just hang in there. The conversation turns towards 'home' and I listen as they both talk about the places where they live. It's very clear that they love this country and the people in their home towns. They're both concerned at how things are changing here and they discuss the different ways that they think they might be able to help the people in their communities to adapt and thrive in the face of this shift.

I make an early start because I want to catch Horler's General Store and Deli on my way out of town just as it opens. They do a mean breakfast sandwich, which is essentially what we'd call a burger, but this one has a fried egg, sausage and bacon. I grab a chocolate bar too as it's going to be a long day. I need to make it about sixteen miles to the next shelter and it's going to be a bit of a mixed bag

– some dry, flat and rock-less easy walking, and a steep one-mile uphill rock fall near the end of the day. I'm optimistic that I'll make it before dark; I can eat up the miles on the good terrain at a pretty reasonable speed, my legs have had a proper rest and I've eaten enough calories over the last couple of days to restore my strength a bit, so that'll help with endurance. Additionally, I have decided to swap out my Injinji toe socks, which I normally wear as liners underneath my Darn Toughs, for my compression socks instead, this should increase circulation and deflect the pain from my heel a bit too. I feel mentally and emotionally renewed and I have made a three to four-day flexible plan, depending on my progress. My head says "I can do this. I will do this".

It's a beautiful day and two miles of it runs through Wallkill National Wildlife Refuge. The path is flat and grassy and there's so much wildlife here. My route takes me around three sides of a square shaped lake. There's a family of Canada geese, complete with a little gaggle of fluffy goslings swimming in the shallows. Not far from them I can see the water moving in an odd manner, as though it's being churned erratically from underneath. I move in for a closer look and see that there are forty, maybe fifty, fat, dark brown, foot-long fish dancing around each other so close to the surface that their backs are sticking out above the water line. They slide past one another in constant motion, weaving and circling; it's fascinating to watch. Black birds with red flecks on their wings sit on the stout tops of large freshwater grasses growing in clumps. I can see some swans gliding gracefully in the open water between the reed beds. Movement in the undergrowth draws my attention, it's a queen snake. These beautiful semi-aquatic reptiles are non-venomous. Their colour can vary a little, this one is a dark brown and has cream coloured stripes running down the length of it. I take a picture of what I think is some kind of duck out on the water, it's a bit too far out to see any detail and it's not until I get home months later and zoom into the dark figure that I realise I have accidentally taken a photo of a beaver out for a morning swim! There is pink honeysuckle, and a weird red flower that looks for all the world like the bottom end of a very fat lady, head invisible and buried, her two legs clad in puffy pantaloons sticking up skywards.

Further on I stop to collect water at a bridge spanning a small creek under the shade of some trees and I decide to make it my lunch stop too. I'm aware that even though I know I still have a way to go, I am not in the least bit anxious, in fact I feel pretty peaceful. I'm not in a hurry today, I don't feel the need to rush. I just know I'm going to get to where I'm going. I check my phone and realise I have good cell service so I WhatsApp call one of my daughters for a chat, she says that I am sounding happier than I have been for a while.

Pochuck Boardwalk is just shy of a mile long, it's a broad and wheelchair friendly raised wooden walkway through wetlands. I walk along it and cross a wooden bridge that sways a bit and appears to be suspended over a shallow river by what look like taut, thick wires. Eventually I come to a muddy field of cows, I navigate my way to the road on the other side by using a line of planks that have been laid down to make a track through the centre of it. The cows seem to know that it's for hikers and stay away. I'm really glad about this because I've always eyed cows with suspicion; I think their apparently docile demeaner is a ruse to lull you into a false sense of security. It probably comes from an encounter I had with a herd of bullocks some years ago. I was out with a friend on a recce for a youth group walk the following week and, convinced that we were on the right track, we climbed over a gate to walk through a field. The bullocks were at the far end and my friend, a Duke of Edinburgh award instructor who had lots of experience walking through fields of cows, was absolutely certain that the animals would ignore us. They absolutely didn't. They came galloping across the open grass towards us at break neck speed. I do not think that I had ever before or have ever since vaulted a gate so fast in my life, it was an Olympic standard leap.

The trail goes straight over the road and begins to climb towards the start of the Stairway to Heaven but I decide to detour to the Heaven Hill Farm and Garden Centre a few hundred yards down the road first. I've been told that they do awesome apple cider doughnuts and I need to fuel up a bit before tackling the boulder field. It's not far off closing time so I'm lucky they still have some left. I sit on one of the picnic benches outside the place and eat two doughnuts followed by a root beer to wash them down before I continue on my way.

I can see how this rocky path came by its name; the boulders go straight up so you can't see where they end...like they're going all the way up to another world. Although it looks like a whole random mess of large rocks without an obvious path, the route up is in fact quite clear, but it is hard going and uses a lot of energy because it's just like climbing a set of oversized and uneven stairs and it involves stepping high constantly.

As I begin my ascent, I hear the sound of very loud music blaring out from somewhere above me, and it's coming closer. The source turns out to be a mobile phone. The young couple carrying it down the mountain stop to inform me that they were told by a hiker descending the rockfall that he had seen a bear somewhere near the top, so they decided to turn around and come back down rather than risk running into it. They apologise for the noise but explain that they're hoping it will deter the animal. I, on the other hand, don't really care whether I run into a bear or not, this trail has thrown enough scary things at me to make encountering a bear small fry and I reckon I could give even a moody bear a run for its money today. Nevertheless, I err on the side of caution and begin to have a long and loud conversation with this 'imaginary' bear as I climb up the trail. I'm hoping this'll give the creature every opportunity to get itself as far away as possible from what it might think is quite clearly a deranged and unpredictable woman talking to herself. Joking apart, in general a bear would rather avoid a human being unless there are exceptional circumstances, scaring the hell out of one by surprising it is one of those exceptional circumstances. Perfectly understandable. If someone creeps up behind me and taps me on the shoulder, I get a bit cross too…after I've recovered from the fright induced minor coronary that is. The trouble is 'a bit cross' translates into 'rip your head off' when you're a startled bear. So, this bear, if there really is one, will absolutely not be surprised. Concerned for my mental health yes, but surprised - definitely not.

By the time I'm about four fifths of the way up the sugar boost I got from the doughnuts and soda has run out. I'm beginning to flag and I know that I still have four miles to go after I reach the top and I will also have to collect water on the way as there's none available close to the shelter I'm staying at. I really want to get there before dark, particularly if I'm walking through bear territory – meeting one in the dark would be a whole other story. It's late in the evening and out of nowhere, it seems, a guy comes jogging (!) up the mountain behind me. He's burly and fit, he's not carrying a pack or any kind of bag come to that and he's got a set of ear buds in. I'm secretly pleased about this last observation as I'd have been pretty embarrassed if I thought he had heard me babbling away to myself like a crazy. He takes off his head phones and he starts talking to me, asking me about my hike. I find out that he's a local mountain rescue guy. He says he's never walked up this path with a pack on his back and he's impressed that I've made it this far still walking at a reasonable pace and not looking like I'm about to have a heart attack. We carry on talking all the way to the top, he is very encouraging and it helps me to keep going. I forget how worn out I was beginning to feel and I hardly notice the time go by. We part company when the terrain levels out and he heads off along another path.

In the end I arrive at Wawayanda shelter with just

enough time to pitch my tent before the last of the daylight disappears. It's a bit of a full house tonight, there's quite a few blokes in the shelter and tenting. We introduce ourselves to each other and have a bit of a banter, they're a friendly lot and there's a good bit of laughter. Home-school is here and he introduces me to his friend GT. It turns out that GT passed me on the bridge where I was having my lunch earlier today. I cook in the dark and sit on the edge of the shelter platform whilst I eat it, chatting to him. I'm concerned about tomorrow; my paper trail-guide, Awol, describes segments of the route as "challenging" and I ask him if he knows anything about the upcoming miles. I know that New York State is renowned for its rock scrambles and I'm crossing the border tomorrow so I want to get an idea of what I can expect. He's a bit vague and nonchalantly says that it's not so bad, there's one bit with a ladder, he thinks, but we're going north so it'll be up and not down, which is easier. Apparently, it'll be ok, he thinks I'll be fine. He encourages me about what I have managed to achieve so far and I feel a bit more confident after our conversation.

In my tent that night I think about the last few days. If I hadn't had that rest in Unionville, I don't think I would have been able to make the progress I did today. The guy on the Stairway was another one of those 'what are the chances' moments too. He came at just the right time, exactly when I needed a bit of a boost and stuck with me, encouraging me the whole way. It's odd how he went off in the other direction at the top, thinking back on it I don't recall another path there at all and he vanished from sight fairly quickly. Kind of reminded me of the whole Knife's Edge thing a bit. I'm reasonably convinced God sent this guy too. You can write off some stuff as a coincidence but when things keep happening, particularly when I've been asking Him to help me out pretty much constantly on this journey, I don't have any trouble acknowledging that there's something else going on here than pure chance. I thank Him for looking out for me and sending the people I needed, quite literally, into my path.

The morning brings a hot, dry, sunny day. I walk past the end of a large shallow body of water, the gnawed and decayed ends of what must have been fairly large trees stick up out of the water. I'm guessing that this 'pond' was created, and is maintained, by beavers. I'm struck by the beauty of the trees on the bank and their perfect reflections in the clear water. The trail starts to climb again and three miles later I cross over into New York. The border is marked on a rock by an underwhelming white line with N. J. painted on one side of it and N. Y. on the other. From here I gain one hundred feet in less than half a mile and arrive at Prospect Rock, the highest point on the Appalachian Trail in this State. There's a Stars and Stripes flag flying up here and the view is amazing.

It's a long hard day and once again I make it to camp at Wildcat shelter with very little daylight to spare. GT lied - the terrain has been difficult to say the least, and I think "challenging" is another word that has somehow been lost in translation. I am actually black and blue from the knee down as a result of climbing rockfalls all day. I stowed my poles early on when I realised that I would need both hands to haul myself up the near vertical boulder climbs, some of them the height of, I'd say, three storey buildings. I had to take my pack off and shove it up and along in front of me at one point. There was another area where I couldn't make out where the next white blaze was so I started to climb up a steep slope with hardly anywhere to grab a hold or place my feet. I used some bushes growing to the side to gain a bit of purchase before I stopped to re-evaluate - how could anyone possibly have ever climbed up here? I took one last look around before I committed to carrying on up it, knowing that if it wasn't the correct route there was no chance that I was going to be able to come back this way safely. There, off to my left and a lot higher up, was the marker I had been looking for…at the top of a rebar 'ladder' that had been drilled into the rockface. I did a semicontrolled slide down a few feet and headed off in the correct direction. On another occasion I must have left the path briefly and missed a short wooden ladder that was meant to aid decent down some smooth rocks on the ridgeline, I ended up having to hang by my fingertips as I sort of slid-climbed down a small drop instead.

All in all, there were some super sketchy areas, I fell a few times and trod in a stream once and all the while I was being eaten alive by every species of biting insect in North America, none of which understood that picaridin is a bug repellent – clearly they've not read the label. It was impossible to see to climb safely with a bug net over my head so the bruises on my legs are now balanced out by red welts and bumps of varying sizes and itchiness all over my face and arms. I make a mental note to ditch the bottle and get some heavy duty DEET at the next available opportunity. But I *have* seen some spectacular views and little things, like patches of tiny violets growing in the crevices between rocks, have made me smile too.

GT is here tonight and I sling a string of expletives at him for misleading me, in a good-natured way of course. He smiles and makes the point that I did it though, and I have to agree that his tactic of lulling me into a false sense of security actually worked. I made it and I'm pretty pleased with myself. Home-school and Red-beard are also staying here, along with a couple of nurses who started their hike about three days ago, they are already a fair way through their stash of 'weed candies', which apparently are legal in this State. They offer to share but I politely decline; I don't want to be off my head if a bear comes wandering through camp tonight.

In my tent I notice that my feet are still wet and wrinkly from that stream I trod in earlier and they're taking a long time to dry out. My boots are so full of holes now, the soles have chunks of rubber missing, the sides have blown out, and they stink. I really need to think about swapping them out soon. Today was a lot of type two fun. I smile. That's another State down and I didn't die today. I am quite genuinely grateful to be alive.

The next day I walk past Fitzgerald Falls, there's a bridge to cross…when I say 'bridge' I mean several fallen tree trunks randomly piled next to each other spanning a creek. I don't fall in. I see another Queen snake, and a little pond that is full of Green frogs, a common species in the eastern United States but striking nevertheless with their green heads and bronze brown bodies. The remainder of the day is more of the same as yesterday and every bit as demanding. The rock climbs are offset by the beautiful vistas over seas of green trees in every hue and texture far below and stretching for miles. It's very hot, too hot, and the bugs are out in force again, I feel like I have my own personal cloud hovering around my head, adding to my collection of bites.

Near the end of the day I meet a guy coming towards me who's doing a yo-yo, that's where you walk the Appalachian Trail in one direction and then you turn around and walk all the way back again. 2192 miles twice in one year! That's some kind of crazy. Huge respect to the man! I ask him about the terrain ahead. He reckons the boulder climbing dries up and the path goes back to 'normal' after the Lemon Squeezer, a few miles ahead. The Agony Grind is about a mile from where I meet him, I want to know what it is exactly, all I know is that it's steep and it's downhill. He says it's just a big boulder field, no problem…I've heard that before. Perhaps I should just stop asking questions that can only be answered subjectively. I seem to remember that I'd already decided that it's all a matter of perspective…I should probably start listening to myself. My knees and ankle have taken a battering over the last two days, his advice to me is "get off, heal up", but I'm determined to carry on…at least I was until I hit the Agony Grind.

It is indeed a big boulder field, a vertical downhill boulder field, with big boulders. Very big boulders. I can only get down by either turning to face the rocks and lowering myself down backwards or butt scooting, and even then, in some places my legs are still dangling in mid-air and I have to drop. It's hell on my knees and at one point I know that I've over flexed my left knee and then I feel an unnatural internal crunching sensation in the same knee as I drop to the next rock down. I'm thinking "That can't be good", but I somehow manage to make it to the bottom…where I discover that I can hardly stand, much less walk, supporting the weight of my pack. I'm not much better when I take it off. I quickly realise that I'm not even going to make it to a stealth camp site I had in mind as an emergency stop let alone the next shelter tonight. Luckily, I'm standing on NY Route 17, and with no other choice, I end up taking Yo-yo Man's advice and Uber myself to the nearest motel. The Agony Grind sure has lived up to its name today.

CHAPTER TEN
Slack packing and site seeing

I'm sitting in my motel room laughing to myself; the couple next door are having very noisy sex – you can't get much more cliché than that! In an attempt to avoid listening to the interesting sounds and the rhythmic banging on the adjoining wall, I take stock of my injuries. There's been so much rock climbing and so many hills today that I have properly killed my knees, I'm actually a bit concerned about them. Everywhere that there is exposed flesh I look like I've had a run in with a cheese grater, bites galore – most of them scratched raw, there's even one in the corner of my eye that's swollen up a bit. Not a pretty look. I feel as though I ought to offer to have my picture taken for an entomology textbook as a showcase for bite ID. My lower legs have taken on a mottled mosaic of purple and blue and some of the bruises hurt to touch. I'm real beat up. I was so close to getting past the worst of the scrambles too. My impression of New York State so far? Basically, one big swamp punctuated by rockfall cliffs. But there's a permanent grin on my face. I'm stoked at what I've managed to achieve. I have done so much in the last few days that I would never have dreamed of doing. Ever. And I haven't even been that frightened, daunted a few times, stumped occasionally, especially where the white blazes were a bit sketchy, but not really that frightened. I've actually enjoyed myself. Who would have thought I'd be so good at cliff climbing with a forty-pound backpack?? Well, "good" is a generous description, but it's all relative – I'm still in one piece. There were plenty of places today where one false step could have resulted in severe injury…or worse. And I'm still thinking about a plan to enable me to carry on, provided I haven't permanently wrecked my knees.

For now, I'm stuck here. I get the most amazing cannelloni delivered from the pizza place over the road. I can literally see the restaurant from my motel room window but I'm not walking anywhere for the next twenty-four hours if I can help it. Spinach, ricotta and tomatoes, all freshly cooked. I've eaten so much I can hardly move anyway right now. I make a start on my next vlog before I eventually fall asleep.

I have a long lay in and eat last night's leftovers for breakfast. Most of the morning and early afternoon are spent going through my stuff and rationalising everything, interspersed with snoozing. The less I have to carry the easier it will be on my knees. I can't afford to stay here for longer than one more night. There's a place called Stoney Point Centre, it's a multi-faith retreat establishment that offers rooms to hikers for an amazingly good rate, especially for New York as this is one of the more expensive States in the US. I was planning to be there in a few days' time in any case, so I ring them and book a five day stay. They run a shuttle service to the trail head and back so hopefully I'll be able to do some slack packing. Carrying a fraction of the weight on my back than usual will test out the extent of the damage in my knees in a reasonably controlled manner. I'll intersperse this with rest days. I also book a whistle stop guided tour of New York City. I'll be two hours coach journey away from the Big Apple and there's a bus stop in

Stoney Point not far from the Centre that will take me to within two blocks of the meeting point in Manhattan. I'm hoping that after all this I will have recovered sufficiently to carry on. With this in mind, I make an additional preliminary five-day plan from Stoney Point to Pawling, doing mostly low miles. I'll have to stop and re-supply there and see what's what.

In the afternoon I Uber to the nearest Walmart…which is only one mile away…I'm taking this 'resting' thing *very* seriously. Besides, the way my legs are, it would have taken me at least an hour to get there on foot, that's if I'd managed to make it at all. I stock up on more pharmaceuticals and I buy a Milky Way chocolate bar. Back at the motel later I discover to my surprise that it's actually a Mars bar in disguise - nougat and caramel covered in chocolate, definitely a Mars bar if ever I saw one. In the lobby of the supermarket there's an oversized hexagonal structure labelled "Pick up point" with some mechanical lift-cum-turntable inside. Apparently, around here, instead of getting your online grocery order delivered you collect it, but it doesn't look big enough to hold even one person's groceries. Makes me think of the Tardis from Doctor Who – bigger on the inside. I imagine an army of tiny people hidden in the depths of the structure frantically sorting and bagging items at a rate of knots. I also buy a massive quantity of baking soda. This I pour into my boots later that evening in an effort to tame the nauseating odour radiating from them. It seems to have evolved into its own kind of life form – you can almost see the cloud of vapour rising. I imagine tendrils of noxious green and yellow spiralling slowly towards the ceiling and materialising into some antithesis of a genie who takes wishes away instead of bestowing them. My knee is holding up but it's very painful and the spring has gone out of it entirely. I noticed earlier that I couldn't even trot across the road. I make a mental note to leave a bit longer in the future so I don't get pulverised by the ubiquitous super-sized trucks.

I have coffee and a late breakfast at the local Dunkin Donuts and get myself Ubered to Stoney Point by a Muslim guy. I tell him about the Islamic-Jewish-Christian multifaith centre I'm going to and ask him about his faith. He talks about how happy he is in America, how glad he is that he made the decision to move here, and how his religion has not caused him any issues at all, even after 9/11.

My accommodation is basic but clean, it kind of reminds me of a boarding school. There's a good community feel and the food is home grown and home cooked. Result. My dinner tastes amazing. Later that evening I pay a visit to the centre's prayer and meditation room. I have the place to myself and I wander up to the bookcase, I pick up one of the Bibles on the shelf and open it up randomly, it lands on Habakkuk, a short book in the Old Testament. The verse on the page in front of me makes me laugh because it's so ridiculously appropriate: "The sovereign Lord is my strength, He makes my feet like the feet of a deer, He enables me to go to the heights". Yep, that's about the size of it. Thank You for the encouragement God...and Your sense of humour.

I'm tired and a bit dehydrated, but I'm actually happy. It's been a steep learning curve in how to handle not having a clue what's coming next and how to make plans on the fly; seat of my pants stuff. I'm doing ok so far and I really believe that God is looking after me. My knee feels marginally better now that I've got it braced to within an inch of its life, and I pat myself on the back for being sensible and taking a break...of sorts anyway. I hope it holds up tomorrow. I drink as much as I can and I get an early night.

Breakfast is every bit as good as dinner was last night. I WhatsApp video call my granddaughter to wish her happy ninth birthday before getting shuttled to the trail head. I plan to walk eight miles north bound. My pack feels so light and easy to carry with only the days essential items in it even though I have quite a bit of water on board because it's very hot and the sky is cloudless. As I come to the top of a rise, I have a clear view of the monument that sits atop Bear Mountain in the far distance, it's on the other side of a valley which I have to traverse before I can climb up and over it to my pick up point in the afternoon.

Ascending Bear Mountain turns out to be a lot easier than I had expected. Where the path is steep there are steps, but they have been hewn out of the rock and are even and of a manageable height. My knees are coping better than I had hoped too, although now my inner thigh muscles are starting to protest as they compensate but they don't cramp up and I am rewarded by the most breath-taking views when I reach the top. It is so indescribably beautiful up here. There are just enough trees and bushes to perfectly contrast the flat rocks I'm walking over, the greens and greys complimenting each other. In one place there's even a bench with an outlook over miles of nothing but forest stretching out into the distance. The chair back and arms have been artistically created from thin tree branches giving it an organic feel that ties it to the landscape. I see a big fat orb weaver spider. Its body is a montage of orangey brown and it has got to be at least an inch long.

As the path winds along the ridge line, I notice more and more people and when I arrive at the monument itself the place is heaving. It's Saturday and this location is very touristy, lots of foreign voices and many American ones too, day trippers from New York City. It's reminiscent of Canterbury city centre in the summer when the High Street is packed like sardines in a tin with people there to see the Cathedral and take in the history. I grab a Gatorade from the vending machine and walk over to look at the view. It's hazy but I can just about make out the NYC skyline far off in the distance. I pass even more of these sightseers huffing and puffing their way up the myriad steps as I am walking down. The climb from the bottom is over one thousand, one hundred and fifty feet and quite a few of them ask me how far they've got left to go before they reach the top.

Thankfully the steps have all been remade recently and they are broad and shallow, it looks like they've been remodelled specifically with tourism in mind which works well for me as they are so much easier to descend than anything I've tackled recently, but it still takes a long time to reach the bottom.

The path off the mountain emerges onto the waterfront of a large leisure lake, there's even a whole flotilla of pedalos neatly parked at one end awaiting the start of the season proper; nothing seems to get going until Memorial Day around here. I recently listened to a podcast from my home church and in it the pastor described how he imagined chasing Jesus across the Sea of Galilee in one of these, I could just see him peddling furiously to catch up and it makes me laugh out loud. Market stalls line the path bordering the water's edge and I buy a Moon Pie from one of the street vendors. It's like a round chocolate cake burger with sponge on either side of a thick vanilla cream in the middle, and it's incredibly sweet. It reminds me of Wagon Wheels, a chocolate covered biscuit and marshmallow snack I used to eat as a child.

My route leads directly through the Trailside Museums and Zoo, it's free to enter and showcases American wildlife. Many of the animals here have been taken in as rescue cases. I come to the bear enclosure. This is the lowest point on the whole Appalachian Trail at just one hundred-and twenty-four-feet above sea level. The place is a mini version of the park I work in at home and there's a park assistant standing by the bears answering questions for the visitors. I stop to chat to the American version of me, telling her about our brown bears and asking her about their black ones, although these two are in fact more of a gingery brown. Apparently, they come in several different colours depending on which part of the country they come from and the predominant habitat they live in; the more forested the environment, the darker the coat colour. These two are originally from Idaho. Fourteen-year-old brother and sister Pal and Sadie were rescued from a life as illegally owned pets when they were still cubs.

The park is full of people and I meet another thru-hiker from Georgia. He tells me that he recently saw two bears just before Fingerboard shelter, and then he had his bear bag stolen and all his food eaten during the night when he stayed there. It's the shelter I was due to camp at the night I pulled off early after the Agony Grind. I had heard that Fingerboard has a resident 'problem' bear that isn't fazed by people, regularly stealing food and refusing to be deterred and it's caused a lot of issues for hikers over the last few years. I guess I was lucky it wasn't my supplies that got pinched, maybe it was just as well I was forced to stop when I did.

I meet my shuttle driver, Susan, at the western end of Bear Mountain Bridge and she drives me back to Stoney Point. It's been a good day but with a very different feel than any other day on this journey so far. It was very strange to be walking with so many people around me today, I almost felt like I was a tourist myself. Although my knees hurt and I'm walking with a permanent limp, and my legs look like a zebra with the ridiculous quantity of black KT tape crisscrossing them underneath the braces on top, they've held up well considering the climb and descent that I've just put them through.

Back at the retreat, I hear some terrible news. I'm on the ATC mailing list and I've received an email informing me that a segment of the Appalachian Trail in Virginia has been closed to hikers following a serious incident. There's been a stabbing, which I later find out resulted in a fatality. Although I'm almost five hundred miles north of where this took place, I'm still a little rattled. These kinds of events are so rare on the trail, it's a relatively safe place, as far as the threat from other human beings is concerned at any rate. People tend to look out for each other and in the main are a friendly bunch. Still, it is slightly unsettling. I feel for those involved, and for those close to the area for whom the impact must be so much greater than it is for me, being fortunate enough to be some distance away.

Before turning in for the night I consider what to do tomorrow whilst I sit and mend my T-shirt with the last of my black thread, it's taken a battering over the last few weeks and has several holes in it now. I had planned to plug some of the eleven-mile gap southbound back to NY Route 17 but the forecast is for torrential rain. I decide to play it by ear and see what the morning brings.

The predicted weather arrives on schedule the next day, it's hammering down and it's cold. I'm not going out in this; I don't need to put myself through that kind of torture. Wet is a nuisance, cold is uncomfortable, but put the two together and you risk hypothermia. If the miles don't get done and I eventually end up with a gap I can't close because I run out of days here, I'm not going to beat myself up about it. My hike, my rules, I haven't taken on the name of One Speed for nothing. It turns out that I made a wise decision. Later that day a lady hiker, Largo, comes in from Brink Road shelter. She's on a LASH (long ass section hike) and has sustained a very serious knee injury. Even worse, as she was walking out to meet the shuttle driver who went to rescue her, she slipped and fell in a stream and ended up frozen cold and on the verge of hypothermia. The conditions out there are treacherous.

I do some laundry but very little else the rest of the day. At dinner I sit with Largo. All the blokes I've talked to have been lovely but it's nice to have some female company for a change. I tell her about my planned trip to NYC tomorrow. I'm not a big fan of cities. There are too many people, too much noise, and too much frenetic activity, but when I'm this close to some of the world's most famous landmarks I'd be crazy to pass up on the opportunity to do a bit of sightseeing and to be a *real* tourist for the day. I make sure that I'm in bed at a reasonable hour in preparation for tomorrow's early start.

The following day I successfully negotiate my way from

the Port Authority Bus Terminal, where my coach has dumped me in the city, to the rendezvous with my tour bus. I have to walk through Times Square and along some of Broadway, it's a bit surreal being in these places that I have only ever seen in movies and news reports. On the way through I stop to grab a coffee and a New York bagel – well, I kind of had to…just for the cliché, right? The day is amazing, I visit lots of famous places, Strawberry Fields, The Rockefeller Centre, St. Patrick's Cathedral, the Flatiron Building to name but a few. At one point I look up and see a guy hanging out of a window in one of the tall buildings. He's cleaning the glass whilst standing on a ledge with nothing to stop him from plummeting to the ground apart from a bungy cord attached to a belt around his waist. I bet he wouldn't have had a problem going over the Knife's Edge! My guide, J, has a great sense of humour and picks on me mercilessly as the only Brit on the tour. His knowledge of his home city is amazing and he ensures that we stop in all the best locations for photo opportunities; there's a particularly good view of the Empire State building perfectly framed between the skyscrapers. Included is a boat trip that takes me past the Statue of Liberty and under the Brooklyn Bridge. The last stop of the day is Ground Zero. There's a Callery pear tree here known as "The Survivor Tree". It was discovered, broken and virtually dead, under all the rubble after 9/11. It survived against all the odds and now, every year, three of its seedlings are sent as a sign of hope to places around the world that have made it through similar devastating events.

On the coach on the way back I replay the day in my head, I can't quite believe I've just been to New York City. I never imagined that I would ever have been doing this. It certainly wasn't on my itinerary, and there would have been a time not that long ago when I would no way have been confident enough to organise a trip like this on the fly, and by myself. I would have been daunted and regarded something like this as too far away and out of reach.

Apparently, the world is a lot smaller than I thought it was, and I'm a lot braver than I think I am too. I grab a gyro (that's a doner kebab to us English) for dinner on the way back to the centre. I've had an amazing day.

In the morning the weather is still wet and cold but the worst of the downpours have subsided so I decide to hit the trail. Despite the conditions, there are still one or two people out hiking. I meet a couple, Cookie and Short Shanks, and I tell them all about my day in the city yesterday. They are surprised that travelling as a single woman didn't put me off visiting NYC on my own. I'm surprised too. A little later I meet Tin Man briefly, on his way to Maine. All in all, I walk about seven miles. It's not enough to fill in the missing distance, there are still five and a half miles between the road where I pulled off and the point I reached today. I've run out of time here and need to move on northbound in the morning so they will have to remain forever un-walked. I feel ok about it, I've done pretty well considering I could hardly stand up a few days ago.

I've been on the trail eight weeks now. My body has appreciated carrying a lighter load but now I have five days' worth of food on board and my pack feels like it weighs a ton after slack packing. I've made sure that I've only got a short day tomorrow so I hope I'll be ok.

CHAPTER ELEVEN

Pizza tastes better shared...and with a side of encouragement

After breakfast I get shuttled back to Bear Mountain Bridge. This suspension bridge was constructed in 1924 and was the longest of its kind in the world at the time. It's also known as the Purple Heart Veterans Memorial Bridge. It's nearly half a mile long and the AT uses it to cross over the Hudson river. I walk across on the pedestrian walkway. There's a steep climb on the other side and it's really hard work, by the time I get to the top I'm exhausted. It seems as though my trail legs have gone on vacation. One week of taking it easy and eating too much good food and I feel *so* out of shape.

The jury's out on whether 'trail legs' are an actual thing. Some people say that after a while, spending day in day out walking up and down hills eventually becomes miraculously easier as your trail legs develop. Other people say that everything still seems just as difficult, but that as you build up your muscles you become less prone to injury. What do I think? I spent weeks waiting for my trail legs until I decided that they were probably a myth. However, what I didn't realise is that I was getting fitter and fitter and each up and down was becoming less exhausting…so I walked further…and harder. This gave me the illusion that nothing had changed. But it had.

About five miles later I stop at the Appalachian Market on US Route 9. This little deli is right on the trail and is open 24/7 all year round. I buy a Philly steak sandwich for my lunch and, predictably, a root beer. The sub is so packed full of meat that I struggle to eat it all. About half a mile on from there I take a short side road down to the Grayson Spiritual Centre's ballfield which they make available for hikers to tent at. It's a massive field with a Portaloo and a covered, open sided pavilion that has power outlets.

I'm the first person to arrive here and I pitch my tent near the picnic benches not far from the pavilion. Pretty soon after, a guy called Chief arrives, he tells me that he's a retired ranger and fire officer and that he's worked all over the country. Grasshopper from New York turns up next. We chat and share stories whilst charging up our electronics. I'm not overly hungry after that massive lunch and just have a snack for my dinner. A bit later Rabbit and Silver Bullet appear, and then a load of other guys that seem to be travelling together but aren't all that talkative. There's a familiar face here too, Tin Man. I have a long conversation with him and he tells me he's visited some friends recently who have given him some supplies and he shares them out with us. He gives me some packets of electrolyte energy supplements and a miniature bottle of Fireball cinnamon whisky, it's plastic so it won't break and it doesn't weigh much. Nice. I've never even heard of the stuff before, but it sounds like just the sort of thing I'd like, and I save it to drink later. There's a good feel to the place this evening.

Everyone else has all but left in the morning whilst Chief, Tin Man and I are still having breakfast. We talk about the upcoming day; it's going to be a really long one and none of us are looking forward to it. We're headed to Canopus Beach Complex. For the last two miles between the road and the tent site there's a choice of two possible routes. The unofficial path, not recommended for hikers but infinitely easier, is along a busy main road. The other is a difficult rocky shoreline section. We debate the merits of both. The jury's out, we'll play it by ear, I guess. I set off before the other two.

The fourteen miles to the camp site are horrible, lots of demanding ups and downs. I opt to walk the path as I'm not sure I want to risk being squashed by the very fast and frequent traffic roaring along the road and diving out of the way is not really on my agenda. At first it seems like a great decision. A whole section of the trail has been built up to a lovely level walkway, I think it's the legacy from some kind of industry here in the past that probably required a flat level surface to get resources out by some kind of mechanical means. There are some nice steps after that too…but the friendly terrain soon runs out. Even the blue side trail down to the beach front, which feels like it's about a mile long, is difficult. Then, once I'm in the complex itself, it isn't clear where I'm supposed to be camping. Eventually I follow some sketchy directions written up on a board, through the eerily quiet buildings, a long way past the toilet and shower block, to a field that appears to have been located about as far away as you can get from the paying public who will be using this resort later in the season.

It's getting late and there's still no sign of Chief and Tin Man. I'm getting a bit worried by the time they finally rock up. Neither of them has enjoyed the day either. I make dinner and then investigate the wash rooms. I'm amazed to discover that they're unlocked and there is warm water so I clean myself up a bit. Before turning in for the night I sit on the picnic bench with Tin Man and chat, he's also nursing an injury and he's concerned that it might be getting worse. I crack open my whisky and drink about a third of the tiny bottle in tiny little sips. It's the first alcohol I've had since the start of this journey and it feels like a well-deserved treat after the long day. I save the rest. I'm glad that tomorrow is going to be a short day, my legs are telling me that I've overdone it today and I'm wondering whether I'm equal to this whole endeavour at all.

Walking along the next day I'm seriously thinking whether I ought to just call it a day, but I feel that if I quit now, I'll have failed. I don't really want to stop but I'm not sure I want to go on either. I'm one of those people that never do anything out of obligation, because I 'ought to'; I give my time and money freely or I don't give it at all. As soon as anything becomes a chore and not a pleasure, a 'should do' instead of a 'want to', I stop enjoying doing it and ultimately stop doing it altogether. Clearly there are some things in life where there is a certain obligation, say if there's a duty of care or a responsibility for example – like feeding your children or cleaning up cat puke – but even with these you can choose to do it with a good grace and out of love…because you want your children to not die of starvation and your cats to have a happy life in a decent, fur ball free, environment. However, I'm also one of those people who, if they say they are going to do something, do it. I feel conflicted. I'm starting to get the impression that I may be doing this walk because I said I would…so I should, but I'm also thinking that I may be being a bit of an idiot to risk permanently damaging myself by bulling on. I've lost sight of what I want, and I'm focusing on the negatives.

All these things are running through my head, and to be honest I'm probably over thinking it all, when I see a couple whom I've passed twice before on previous days coming towards me. They have a dog that seems to be a bit nervous, and not wanting to upset the animal, I haven't stopped to chat with them before, but for some reason today I decide to say hello. They are Soul Food and Jump Start. They've walked a large proportion of the AT already and are out doing day hikes to cover some of the remaining miles. We talk about how punishing the trail can be and also how neither of us discovered this during our preparatory research; no one ever talks about this aspect of it honestly and we agree that it's very frustrating. I happen to mention my thoughts on whether to continue. They offer to pray for me. It turns out they're Christians. Soul Food speaks some wise words, she says that I need to let go of my expectations of the trail and let God show me what He wants for me. I feel quite emotional, like I've been let 'off the hook', like I have permission to quit or to not quit. That is to say, the pressure that I have been needlessly putting myself under lifts and I realise that I don't actually have to live up to anything – whatever I decide I know I will have made the best effort I could, that I have already achieved so much, learnt so much, and experienced so much. Whatever I decide, it's ok. Obvious really, but sometimes you just need someone looking in to give you a different perspective. I still don't know what I'm going to do ultimately though, I can't make up my mind.

My arrival at the Ralph's Peak Hikers' Cabin, known as the RPH shelter, marks exactly four hundred miles, taking into consideration the five and a half I left out through injury. This shelter used to be a completely enclosed building at one point but one of the walls was taken out and a little veranda built on the end instead. It's got three proper bunk beds and each of them has a basic foam pad. As I look up at the ceiling, I see two disembodied feet, complete with socks and trainers, hanging down as though the owner had stuck his legs through the roof. I laugh. There's lots of space for tenting on the lawn and some actual tent platforms too but I decide to nab one of the bottom bunks, I'm half thinking I might take a zero here tomorrow.

Chief arrives but he only stops for a short while, he needs to move on as he's got a package to pick up in a town further up the trail so he's on a clock and needs to meet his deadline. Tin Man turns up too. He is really concerned about the flare up of his previous injury. His daughter lives close enough for him to decide to pull off and visit with her to give his body a chance to recuperate. Before she arrives to pick him up, we have a conversation and I tell him that I too am thinking of quitting. Because I don't live in the States, I can't just have a month's proper break – it would cost me a fortune in motels, even an Airbnb would probably bankrupt me for that amount of time. He encourages me by telling me that he thinks I'm "as hard as nails" and that if I really want it, he thinks I could be capable of doing it. He's right, I'm a pretty determined character. I guess that's it though isn't it? Where's my mind at? Why am I here? What's my attitude like? Some days are good, some days I resent each up and each down. What's that all about? Is this trail a mind game? I think a lot of it is, and that is exactly what is keeping me here…but I can't will a busted limb to walk hundreds of miles.

The place starts to get busy in the afternoon, the bunks quickly fill up and tents start to appear. The good thing about this shelter is that it's very close to a road and there's a pizza place that will deliver here. I club together with three other guys and we order a large cheese and tomato pizza each and a couple of large bottles of Coke to share. When they arrive, they are massive! I quickly realise that there's no way I can eat all of mine.

It's getting towards evening when I see a couple of ladies turn up and start pitching their tent. I walk over and ask them if they'd like to come and share my meal in a bit. They introduce themselves as No Name and Splash. We eat and chat, they're really good company and I like them straight away. It seems as though I've started something and the other guys, who were going to save their left overs for breakfast, end up sharing their food too. Everyone there gets something to eat and there's a community atmosphere, a buzz about the place.

After dinner the ladies offer to make me a cup of tea, it's a lovely gesture and I really appreciate their kindness. I talk to them about my journey so far, and explain that the reason for my adventure is to mark my fiftieth birthday year. I mention my dilemma, wondering if I should keep going. No Name comes up with a brilliant suggestion, she says why not try for "500 for 50". I think it's a wonderful idea. It seems like a reasonable goal, and it would give meaning to my walk with the 'fifty' – one hundred miles for every decade of my life. Elegant. I'm encouraged and suddenly feel enthusiastic again. There is a good reason to carry on and a definite distance to aim for. An end in sight…but one with no connotations of failure. I feel like I've made a positive choice and taken back control of my journey.

In the morning I meet a couple of work colleagues from NYC and one of their sons out for a weekend hike. The father and son are originally from England but settled here some years ago. They don't have trail names and I later jokingly suggest "Tetley" for one of them as he sits and drinks his tea. I leave before them but they soon draw level at the top of a very steep climb. We end up yo-yoing around each other all day. About lunch time I catch up to the girls, they've picked up food from the Mountaintop Deli half a mile off the trail. I decide that that's a pretty good idea and take the detour myself, where I grab a Gatorade, another massive sub and a chocolate bar.

Towards the end of today's very hot nine miles, there's a rock scramble 'end of day curve ball'. I'm pleased that my knees hold up reasonably well, considering. The ladies and the NYC boys are all here at the Morgan Stanley shelter along with a couple of others. I get some help from one of the guys to hang my bear bag; I'm still not that good at it. I collect water from an old iron water pump down a slope from the shelter site. No Name quickly and efficiently builds a fire and we sit around the picnic bench to the side of the fire pit chatting into the evening. They're all telling me that I'm doing good to have got to four hundred miles and to still be here. I really value their encouragement and I'm feeling grateful to be surrounded by such positive people, it makes a massive difference to my state of mind, which in turn makes a massive impact on my ability to keep going. I'm beginning to realise that, provided you aren't injured out, the secret to conquering this trail is to set your mind right.

It was a hot night and I'm going to have to pay attention to my water consumption today, and make sure I get enough electrolytes as it's going to be a sweaty eleven miles, I'm guessing. The girls leave before me. I'm going to miss those two, they were such a big encouragement to me. I tell them about my YouTube channel so they can keep up with my progress…and have a laugh. I'm the next to leave but the boys catch up and overtake me. I see them later at the edge of Nuclear Lake having their lunch. Apparently, the lake isn't actually 'nuclear' any more, although it might have been once; there was an explosive incident involving a nearby plutonium research facility in the seventies. It's HOT today but I'm enjoying the walk. In places, what look like six to eight-foot-high jasmine bushes line the path, they smell heavenly and there's even some flat, boarded terrain. I pass the Appalachian Trail train station, the only one on the AT. Trains from here run to and from NYC. It's simple but pretty. There are two sets of yellow steps leading to a small open raised area with a green bench that has a notice board either side.

I emerge onto NY Route 22 and walk just short of a mile to Tony's Deli. I was planning on tenting here for the princely sum of two dollars for the night but there's a severe weather warning for thunder storms in place for Pawling tonight. I need a light resupply in any case, and my shoes are dying so badly now that they are killing my feet, so I use my better judgement and pull off for the night. Connecticut is less than seven miles away and a fraction of the price of New York State so I get a cab over the border to New Milford and check into a cheap motel.

There's no storm in the night but the air is thick and exceptionally hot and muggy in the morning, I'm betting the promised thunder is on its way. Well, whatever the weather decides to do I have *got* to get a new pair of boots today. There are surprisingly few outfitters along the AT, and those that are at a viable distance from it don't always hold stock with hikers in mind. Kent is just a few miles up the same road I'm staying on and it has a shoe shop with a very good reputation.

Kent is a beautiful little town. The welcome sign tells me that it was established in 1739. At the centre there's a green space with interesting sculptures. Two large, semi-see-through whale tail fins stick up out of the ground in a 'V' shape, they're made from strips of intertwined silver metal that makes me think of the lattice work on a pie top. There's a super-sized family of blobby people lounging on the grass sculpted in the style of 'Morph', a stop motion character made out of modelling clay from a children's TV series in the seventies. A life-sized metalwork hiker, complete with backpack, stands outside the welcome centre, which has showers around the back. It feels like a friendly and hospitable place.

I've packaged up some more of my gear that I need to send home now that the temperatures are consistently higher at night and I mail these from the local post office. Then I make my way down the main street to Sundog Shoes. I tell the guy behind the counter that I am from Kent too – the county of Kent in England. We chat as I try on various boots and insoles to go in them. He's super helpful, he even offers to ditch my old, smelly, busted boots, which I think is very gracious of him as after only five minutes with them sitting next to me on the floor, a cloud of choking odour has already started to make a take-over bid for control of the atmosphere in the store. I'm really happy with my purchase and as I walk out of the shop with them on my feet, I'm feeling hopeful that I'll be ok wearing them without breaking them in gently first.

On the recommendation of the shoe shop guy, I visit Kent Coffee and Chocolate Co., and I'm not disappointed. They have a huge array of amazing cakes, chocolates, and ice creams, it smells wonderful in there and it's hard to choose what to have. I get a coffee and an Oreo cupcake. The staff are very friendly and when the waitress finds out that I'm an AT hiker she gives me an enormous chunk of seed, fruit and nut cake for free and offers to fill up my water bottles for me.

I have to wait twenty minutes for my ride back to New Milford so I wander over to the hot dog stand to grab a root beer and talk to the vendor, Chris, whilst I wait. An old retired army guy on his bike comes over to join us, he's picked up a dollar bill that had blown across the road in front of him when the hot dog man dropped it accidentally whilst fishing out the change for a customer. It prompts a long conversation about honesty and how it's a rare attribute these days. After I leave Kent, I head to the local Walmart to get some supplies. The sky's been getting darker and as I leave, the heavens open. It chucks it down, like I could wash my hair in it it's that heavy. I'm so glad I wasn't caught in a tent in this.

Later I get a message from No Name, they've been having a laugh at some of my Vlogs. They offer to hike into the nearest shelter just before I hit my five hundredth mile so they can celebrate it with me. I'm touched by their proposal and quite excited. I make a few preliminary plans and the time frame and location look doable. I'm looking forward to sharing the moment with them; it seems right and fitting. I suppose I ought to start thinking about what I'm going to do after that.

CHAPTER TWELVE

A Cat called Socks and lots of goodbyes

I'm back on the trail by nine in the morning and I stop off later at Wiley shelter to have my lunch. On the way I meet Amtrak, she smiles and says, "Not interstate. Like the local train service, because I stop often." She tells me that she's finishing up a section that she wasn't able to complete on her thru-hike attempt two years ago because her feet gave up on her. They got to the point where the nerves were so affected by the constant demands of the trail that she was in danger of permanent damage if she didn't stop.

Seven miles into the day and a friendly green notice board welcomes me to Connecticut, "Gateway to New England", but I haven't left New York State for the last time yet though; there's a small section coming up that'll take me back there temporarily for a couple of miles. I arrive at Ten Mile River shelter at half past four after a knee busting seven-hundred-foot steep drop in elevation. But, to be fair, it was a nice day and the walking was ok...mostly.

I have seen a lot of wildlife today. I passed a pond that had an army of American bull frogs basking in the shallows. I saw a couple of unusual birds, one of them was an enormous woodpecker the size of an owl! It had a red head and a long spindly neck that made it look like one of those old-fashioned kids' toys where you had to 'ping' the bird at the top of a wobbly metal rod to set it in motion so it 'pecked' its way to the base. The other was an extremely well camouflaged small, hooded, pale bellied bird with a darker back and a light outline around its eyes. It was ferreting around in the undergrowth in the woods. I managed to take a photo and, I can't be sure, but I think it might have been a Connecticut warbler, apparently, they are notoriously difficult to spot. The highlight of the day though was my first wild bear sighting! It was so far away that it looked the size of a matchbox car on the top of a rise in a sparsely wooded area, but it was unmistakably a bear. I was so ridiculously excited!

It looks like I'm on my own at Ten Mile River shelter. I cook and have eaten my dinner when a young couple turn up, I won't be here alone tonight after all then. It's late and I'm very tired so, after a quick "hello", I retire to my tent for the night.

In the morning, I realise that it's only one month until my fiftieth birthday and, although I was planning on spending it on the trail, now I think that really and truly I'd probably rather spend it with my friends and family back home in England. I'm missing them.

Today I only walk just shy of eight and a half miles…but they're a nightmare. Lots of rocks, lots of scrambling, lots of pointless ups and downs where the trail could so easily have been routed around the base of short, difficult to negotiate rocky rises, *and* I've not seen a soul all day. My legs aren't doing what I ask them to and keep buckling when I bend them beyond a certain angle as I step down, and I'm relying heavily on my poles to take my weight when I walk downhill. By the time I roll into Mt. Algo shelter I am miserable and exhausted, but at least there is someone here to talk to.

It's an older bloke with a long beard and who looks like

he's been living in the woods permanently for quite some time. It's one of those situations where I have to make a snap decision, a judgement call on whether I think this guy is 'safe' to spend the night around or whether to move on to the next shelter or at least a tent site further on. I decide he's ok and I'm really glad I do; I don't know it yet, but he helps me with a plan for my last few days in America after I finish on the AT. He seems nice enough; likeable and quite a character. I sit with him to eat my lunch and later to cook and eat my dinner, in between we talk. I note that he's got a bit of a stutter, but after a while, I don't notice it any more. His name is Uncle Walt and he's taken a zero here today. He says he spends six months of the year out in the woods. He's from New York but he's currently making his annual pilgrimage to see his brother in Vermont.

As I sit in my tent that night, just before the light fails, I see a tick climbing up the outside of the mesh on the upper part of my tent. I quickly spray it with DEET and it drops off. I'm really glad that I used my amazingly versatile and extraordinarily sticky tenacious tape to repair a small hole that had appeared a few days ago on the ridge at the top of the tent. It could easily have crawled through there and dropped down onto me in the night. So far, my tick lasso hasn't had to come out of its packet and, if I can help it, I'd rather it didn't have to. I make a mental note to choose where I pee when I get up in the dark carefully and to try and avoid any trees near taller areas of undergrowth.

Before I fall asleep, I remember the beautiful deep pink lady slipper orchid I saw today. I've never seen one before and the bloom was much bigger than I had expected it to be. It was beautiful, and it really did look like a fat toed velvet slipper, even the two leaves just above the flower brought to mind delicate laces for tying it to a lady's slim ankle. The AT might throw curve balls at you, but it always gives you gifts to lift your spirits too, almost by way of an apology for its harsh demands. Since I've been out here there's been something to smile about, to be thankful for, pretty much every single day, regardless of how I've felt. Whether it's been the views, the flora and fauna, or just the people I run into, I've always had a reason to focus on the positives. They may seem like little things, but I choose to give them more credence. For all their tiny size, I pay them the most attention and give them the highest weight in my mind – these are the things the trail is about, these are the things that I am determined to take home with me from this adventure.

In the morning, I leave before Uncle Walt. I have ten miles to walk and they should take me over Caleb's peak - a difficult, steep rocky ascent and descent, and over St. John's Ledges - 'steps' down a rocky cliff similar to the Agony Grind but more demanding. I make an executive decision and bypass both of these in favour of a riverside trackway that meets back up with the AT further along. I know that I don't have the physical capability to tackle either of these currently, and I'm not even going to try; today is not going to be the day I get airlifted off a mountainside.

The path into Stewart Hollow Brook shelter is wide, rock free, flat and beautiful. The sun glints through the trees on either side and every so often I can see the river I'm walking parallel to. For the first time ever, there is no curve ball at the end of the day. I pitch my tent where I can see and hear the Housatonic river through the trees. It's peaceful here. My mind is clear and I make a decision – I can't walk any more of this terrain safely in my present state. Every time I see a rock field, stream or a steep elevation I break out into a cold sweat – I don't trust my knees not to give in on me. I can cope with any amount of pain, but now I'm genuinely frightened that I might fall and seriously injure myself through the mechanical failure of my anatomy, and with very good reason. I've had to use my poles as crutches when my knees have given way more than once, these poles are not really designed for this and are showing signs of weakness now. My mind and body agree that I have done enough. People say "never quit on a bad day" – today has not been a bad day.

There's a short flat section a few miles ahead, if I walk that, I'll have done four hundred and fifty miles. It's not "500 for 50" but it is still a good solid number, and the 'fifty' makes sense – four hundred plus one mile for every year of my life. I'm not sure I want to go home yet, but I have no idea what I will do next, beyond, hopefully, spending a week at a hostel in Lakeville, Connecticut, to heal up a bit. For now, I have drawn an important line in the sand and I'm pleased with what I've done. I'm proud of myself for ploughing through some significant personal challenges, I've met some awesome people, and I'm glad I came.

I let No Name and Splash know what I've decided. I'm disappointed that our plans to meet won't come to fruition, and I feel a bit like I've let them down, but they're so kind and encouraging and still want to meet up before I leave. That night I have a good cry, it's as much from relief that I have made a choice as it is from sadness that my adventure is drawing to a close.

I still feel confident of my decision in the morning. I'm going to spend a whole day zeroing here. It's beautiful and I need the head space before I move on. Uncle Walt is here too and he's also decided to zero, we chat on and off throughout the day. It turns out that he's done a lot of travelling on foot in the past and he gets out one of the maps he's carrying. It's of the Chesapeake and Ohio (C & O) Canal Path, one hundred and eighty-four and a half miles in total, running from Cumberland, MD, to Georgetown, DC. It passes through Harpers Ferry and it's sixty miles from there to Washington. This trail is essentially a bike route but people do walk it. There are "hiker/biker" camp sites at manageable intervals *and* it's absolutely flat. No hills. No rocks. No mountains. Flat. I can do flat. My enthusiasm gathers and I start making some plans.

It's Memorial Day weekend and there are lots of people here tonight. There's one lady hammocking, I have to ask her how her name is spelt because when spoken with a US accent it could be either "Hostel" or "Hostile". She smiles and says that's kind of the point. She got given her name after she had a bit of a run-in with someone at a hostel earlier on her journey. She's a pleasant and out-going character and I can't imagine her having a serious barney with anyone. Sisters June Bug and Butterhead are also here, they recognise me from a little while ago when we passed each other briefly but I can't remember exactly where on the trail that was – I do know that we were walking in opposite directions at the time though, and now we are all travelling north. June bug is walking with a bit of a limp, her ankle has sustained an injury. By the looks of things, I think it's probably a lot worse than she's letting on. These two also had a run in with the rogue bear at Fingerboard shelter, they only managed to hang on to their supplies because one of them was carrying a bear barrel. There are bear tooth marks on June Bug's drinking mug; what a cool memento to take home from her journey!

Quite a few of us are gathered around the picnic bench talking and I'm asked what the actual date of my fiftieth birthday is. We discover that three of us share identical birth dates, just on different years – June Bug, Uncle Walt and me. What are the chances of that happening amongst a crowd of strangers? We take a selfie to commemorate the occasion.

I'm the last out of camp in the morning. I have planned my whole day around food. There are three places I can stop to eat today and I plan to indulge myself to celebrate surviving the AT. I walk slowly down the trail along the riverside towards Cornwall Bridge, about four miles away, where I plan to breakfast at the Cornwall Country Market store and deli. I turn off the path about two and a half miles beyond the shelter and join a single-track road. Very soon after that, a John Deere Gator slows down next to me. Bruce and his grandson are out for a little jolly and they kindly offer to give me a ride to the main road, so I climb into the open cargo box at the back. I've never travelled in the back of a truck before, it's actually fun and very cool. I tell him my story and mention one of the places I'm hoping to eat at today – The Mountainside Café. It turns out that he's one of the people who runs it and he gives me a bit of history. It's a place that's been set up to champion local produce, support the surrounding community, and to give the staff, who are individuals in recovery, the opportunity to gain some experience and life skills to help them with their sober lifestyle. I think it's a wonderful idea and I'm glad that I've earmarked it for a visit.

When we get to the main road, I hop off, wave goodbye and walk the short distance to the deli. Uncle Walt is already there having his breakfast and I order a wrap and a coffee. As I'm tucking into my food, four of the other hikers who stayed at the shelter last night also turn up. One of their number, Lynn, isn't walking on with them today and has picked up her vehicle to give the others a lift back to the trail. She's going in our direction and generously drives Uncle Walt and me the seven miles to the Mountainside Café on US Route 7. For my lunch here, my second food stop of the day, I have a root beer float and a chicken salad, and I also charge up some of my electronics and book my hostel stay at Lakeville. When I'm done, I cross over the road and follow a blue blaze track that's virtually opposite the restaurant back to the AT.

I come across a couple of younger guys, one of them looks pretty rough, they've been on the trail for only two days and already the pointless ups and downs of the Connecticut portion of the AT have started to kill his knees. I don't think it's just his knees that are making him look ill though, it's been hot and I think he might be dehydrated; it is so easy to forget to drink enough to mitigate all that sweat. Without enough water your legs cramp up, your joints don't work efficiently and you begin to feel very lethargic and hot. I advise him to drink as much as he can at the next available opportunity.

A bit further up the path, I catch up to Uncle Walt and

we walk into Falls Village, Canaan, together. As I turn onto the road at the trail head, I see what I think will be my last white blaze, it's quite an emotional moment. We make our way to the Toymakers Café for an early dinner. The owner is a British motorbike enthusiast so there are little reminders of home around the place, Union Jacks, a London underground map, even the mini free-library outside is in a scaled down model of a red phone box. I buy a veggie soup and a birch beer. Whilst I wait for my meal, I pick up the half-done Rubik cube that's on the table in front of me and complete it. I haven't picked one of those up for a while, it reminds me of my teenage years, and it's nice to know I haven't forgotten how to solve it.

Uncle Walt heads off to the camp site behind the local power station. I say farewell to him for the last time. It's so sad that you have the privilege of meeting all these people on the trail, and as soon as you start to get to know them, you're saying goodbye, and you're probably never going to see them again. I sit on the bench outside and watch the birds that are brave enough to land on the grass to pick up the titbits of food accidentally left behind by the messy diners, now that it's quiet and they've all gone home. There are American robins, ubiquitous starlings, a pair of cardinals and several blue jays. Trying to get some good photographs of them keeps me occupied until Cory, the owner of the hostel in Lakeville, arrives to pick me up.

The hostel is in fact a whole house and I have my own room too! It's a quaint red brown weather boarded place with a stream running alongside the property. I can hear the water gurgling through the open window of my bedroom, I smile because the sound gives me the illusion that I'm still tenting in the woods. The building was made into a home from an empty shell many, many years ago by her other half's father, although they themselves don't live here now; a resident caretaker looks after the place. Everything inside is handcrafted; it has a wonderful old-world charm to it and it feels comfortable and cosy. I love it.

Another good thing is the cat. She's called socks and we fall in love with each other pretty much straight away. She sits on my lap whenever I'm still for more than five minutes, and even tries to sneak into my room at night by pushing the door open and I have to barricade it with my walking boots. I've had cats since I moved into my first property when I was eighteen years old and at one point, I shared my house with seven of them…that's another story in itself. I had no choice but to sell up last year and the rented place I moved into wouldn't accept animals so I had to re-home the last remaining one, a nineteen-year-old little lady. She settled into her new home well, but I was devastated and felt guilty about abandoning her in her old age. So, having a cat to love and pet here is a big deal, it's kind of therapeutic and she somehow helps me to deal with the loss of mine.

What isn't good are the stairs…well, not the actual stairs themselves, there's nothing wrong with those…it's my inability to climb them. This is the first time I've had to tackle normal stairs since my knees got bad, and without my poles to aid me I find myself having to go up them on all fours and coming down is much worse. I knew they were bad, but I really had no idea they were *this* bad. I'm thinking that I was very wise to pull off when I did because if I'd pushed it any further, I reckon I'd have been in a whole world of trouble and quickly become my own liability.

I get up late the next day and slowly walk to On the Run, the local coffee shop that's literally two minutes' walk up the road, for a breakfast bagel and a good coffee. It's a small but pleasant place and I people-watch as I eat and drink. The staff seem to know every single person who walks through the door, whether they're just popping in for a takeout or sitting down, and the customers all seem to know each other too. My impression of the whole village is that it's a close-knit community where they take care of each other and take a great deal of pride in their surroundings. It has a friendly atmosphere and they seem to be pretty welcoming of visitors too. As I walk around, I feel as though I've been transported into an episode of the Gilmore Girls, the houses and landscaping look so similar it could easily be Stars Hollow.

Behind the hostel there's a flat, mile and a half long track going all the way to Salisbury. It's called the Railroad Ramble and it used to be part of a line run by the Central New England Railroad who stopped using it in 1967. It's a beautiful walk through a mixture of trees and some more open areas including a large pond with a bench located at just the right spot to enjoy it. I visit the supermarket in Salisbury and grab some supplies for the next few days and I eat my lunch at a proper wooden garden table, on a proper wooden garden chair – no cheap and nasty picnic benches here, this is *quality* garden furniture. Not only that, but there's an actual power outlet on the side of the supermarket building under the village notice board for anyone to use free of charge. Opposite that is a free mini-library. I'm loving rural Connecticut more and more…I could happily live here I reckon, so I'm not surprised when I'm told that Meryl Streep and Kevin Bacon have both owned properties near here and that Rip Torn owns one of the houses along the road where I'm staying. Every time I visit the super market here in the next few days I keep my eyes peeled for celebrities.

Back at the hostel, Cory pops in with coffee and cookies, we enjoy a good long chat about politics, the trajectory that America is on, and life in general. The rest of the afternoon is spent playing with Socks between booking my flight home and my accommodation in DC at either end of my upcoming canal walk, and catching up with No Name and Splash. They're going to drive the two hours from their home just to meet me for breakfast in a couple of days' time so that they can see me before I leave. I'm overwhelmed that they would want to do that, and I'm really looking forward to seeing them again.

It's Monday and it's Memorial Day, and there's a lovely surprise – Cory comes through the door, closely followed by June bug and Butterhead! It's great to see these familiar faces and I'm very happy to learn that they're staying for a few days but the reason for their stay isn't so good – June Bug's ankle. Cory happens to be a doctor and takes a look at it and at my knee also. She generously takes a trip to fetch some supplies for us – compression bandages and arnica gel. Injury notwithstanding June bug seems to be in relatively good spirits. They recount the events that led them here when they decided to pull off the trail, it isn't a funny story really but the way they tell it looking back on it is absolutely hilarious. I understand how she must have felt completely. They have both done so amazingly well, even with her injury she still walked over the top of Caleb's Peak and descended St. John's Ledges. I take my hat off to her – that was brave!

I'm trying to keep moving to prevent my knees from seizing up so I walk to the lake that's just beyond the coffee place and sit in the sunshine for a bit. Later in the day I trundle up the railway track and sit on the bench by the pond and just chill. For dinner, June Bug treats us to a takeaway meal from Mizza's Pizza. It's only up the road next door to On the Run, but none of us want to walk up there this evening. It's lovely sitting around the table together, and I wish I'd had the opportunity to walk with these two on the trail.

The next day is pretty uneventful. June Bug makes some amazing American pancakes for breakfast and we get dinner delivered again because the weather's a bit rough. In between I laze around and, every so often, I put a few pieces into the jigsaw puzzle we've got on the go.

Wednesday morning and I'm not dining on my own – No Name and Splash have driven down to meet me for a breakfast date. It's *so* good to see them. They have a real heart for people, and for introducing them to hiking. They're very encouraging, and they're right, I *did* do good, and I am *so* grateful that they persuaded me to continue when I was thinking of quitting at four hundred miles. I would have felt disappointed in myself, as if I'd walked away by default rather than by choice, and this way I'm finishing strong – on my terms. As we talk and I share about my plans, I realise that I'm not done with hiking yet and I think that I might seriously consider coming back and doing a bit more of the AT when I'm back in shape. But for now, I'm going to have to make do with walking along a flat canal path. By the time I finish that I'll have walked five hundred miles here after all. Before they drive home, I introduce them to June Bug and Butterhead. They've walked different sections of the trail than each other and they swap some useful info. I give them a big hug and say farewell.

I finish the jigsaw in the afternoon and upload my last AT vlog. June Bug and Butterhead have been tidying up and cleaning for something to do to alleviate the boredom that comes with having to rest an injured foot. It's a bit chilly outside and there's lots of rain again this evening so tonight we order in burgers and fries. They're really good. Then we gather around June Bug's phone to watch a couple of episodes of Miss Fisher's Murder Mysteries on Netflix before we turn in for the night. I've got one more full day here. It's going to seem a bit strange to be living on the road again.

After breakfast I take a walk to the store in Salisbury to sort out a few supplies because I'm going to be travelling most of the day tomorrow. I see two Meryl Streep lookalikes whilst I'm there. Back at the hostel we end up talking about plants and gardens, I guess they call them 'yards' here. I show the ladies pictures of my 'large', by UK standards anyway, garden in the village I lived in before I sold my house. The fruit and vegetables I grew in it, along with an allotment plot nearby, provided almost all the produce we needed for the whole year. As I look at the photos, I feel a bit emotional, and I realise how much I miss it…and how much I've been avoiding thinking about how much I miss it.

Our evening meal is every bit as good as the previous

ones. I'm sad it's the last. I reckon the cat is going to be devastated when I leave, we'll be lost without each other. My pack is about two pounds lighter after I ditch even more surplus stuff into the hostel's hiker box, and it does actually feel lighter. 6am start tomorrow. Cory's coming to give me a lift to the station for the first leg of my three-hundred-and-forty-mile journey back to DC.

CHAPTER THIRTEEN
Back to the beginning

The ladies have already brewed the coffee ready for me in the morning. They're kind, funny and generous, and I've really enjoyed the time we've spent together over the last few days, it's felt like a real 'home'. I've relaxed, my body has recovered a bit from the battering it's had, and I feel charged up to embark upon the next leg of this adventure. It's like I'm marching into the unknown again. The logistics of just getting to my starting point in Harpers Ferry from where I am are a bit daunting. I hope I find my way around and make all my connections without any major issues. I reckon I'll be ok, I'm pretty good at thinking on my feet when I need to. On the way to the station, Cory talks about her family, her life, and her past. It's really interesting listening to her and I wish I could have spent more time getting to know her a bit better.

Wassaic station is just over the border in New York. I catch the 6.48am train into NYC and manage to book my Greyhound ticket from there to Washington DC whilst I'm still sitting on the train. I arrive later at Grand Central, which is just that – grand. It's one of the top tourist attractions in the world and if one travel website's survey is to be believed, it had over twenty-one million visitors in one year, and that's not including the people who were there to actually use it as a station! In fact, it's *so* grand that its contribution to America's cultural and historical heritage was recognised in 1976 when it was awarded the designation of "National Historic Landmark". There's a lot of marble everywhere. The design is from a time long-gone, and if you were just looking at the architecture, you'd never peg it for a railway station, but it was built in 1913 so I guess in those days it was less about utility and more about bling and the wow factor. I walk the few blocks to the Port Authority Bus Terminal on 42nd and 8th. I've been here before not so long ago and I know exactly which way to go and I'm amused by how confidently I'm striding through the busy streets of this big city even though I'd never set foot in the place until a few weeks ago. My route takes me past the New York public library and I notice that beneath my feet there are plaques embedded in the pavement, each one with a quote engraved on it. One in particular draws my attention: "The universe is made of stories, not of atoms".

I catch my Greyhound late morning. I've noticed that the security in this country seems to be ridiculously tight, they won't even let the passengers onto the bus without seeing their photo ID first. There's a couple of ladies who've turned up late and try to bypass the queuing system for the allocated seat numbers. The inspector, also a woman, isn't having any of it. There's a mini verbal fracas and I'm expecting a full blown cat-fight to ensue, claws 'n' all. Thankfully, the other passengers and I are saved from a fisticuffs showdown. I'm really glad that I brought my driver's licence, I don't want to mess with this tough cookie. The bus goes under the Hudson river through the Lincoln tunnel. I'm pretty certain that I once watched a post-apocalyptic film where someone had to walk over myriads of dead bodies in here. I can see exactly why this location was chosen to feature in a horror movie. It's a mile and a half long and one hundred feet underground, and without the headlights of the moving vehicles or electricity it would be a mighty scary place to negotiate. I don't think I'd fancy it myself. I'd keep imagining all those dead bodies re-animating and turning into brain eating zombies.

...And before I know it, we're on the New Jersey Turnpike. I never knew that 'turnpike' meant toll road, and I had no idea this one was so long – over 180km. Looking out of the window I can see the New York City skyline disappearing into the distance behind me. I might not have boarded *my* Greyhound in Pittsburgh, but it's still on the same route that Cathy and her lover took in Simon and Garfunkel's song, and now *I'm* counting the cars on the New Jersey Turnpike, "they've all come to look for Ameeeee-ri-ca." The journey takes a few hours. I cross over the Delaware and Susquehanna rivers for the second time and I think back to when I first crossed them. I realise just how far I've come on foot, and just how much water has flown under the bridge, metaphorically...and literally, since then.

The bus drops me round the back of Union Station, and I walk to Hostel International. Later that evening I stock up on food for the next few days and then rearrange my backpack in the morning after breakfast to accommodate it all. I check out, and then I head back to Union Station to buy my ticket to Harpers Ferry for later that day. There's only one train that stops there each day and I want to make sure that I have a seat on it. There are a few hours before it departs though, so I take a short walk to the Capitol. This imposing looking structure is home to the United States Congress, and paradoxically, the District of Columbia's residents have no meaningful representation in the House of Representatives and none at all in the Senate. This is because, apparently, it's not an actual State, only a district. Bit rough that, doesn't seem fair to me. I do a bit of touristy walking around, taking pictures of the impressive building. Just as impressive, to me at any rate, is a bold little sparrow that hops around so very close to my feet waiting for me to drop him a few crumbs from the bagel I'm eating for my lunch.

As I wait in the queue for the train later, I see a large family of Mennonites, or at least I think that's what they are. The ladies have matching home-made plain and simple, utilitarian dresses cut from a drab coloured fabric, and on their heads, they wear white bonnet style hats. The men are wearing braces to hold up their trousers and black wide brimmed hats, all of them have distinctive matching facial hair. They remind me of the characters from the seventies TV series, Little House on the Prairie. I look down at their feet. I can see that they're wearing regular, off the peg, commercially manufactured trainers and it makes me a bit sad that even though they're holding on to some aspects of their culture, modernity has begun to creep in and erode their traditional identity.

The train is impressive. I'm on the top deck and I've got an amazing amount of leg room, like masses of it. I can put my pack in the footwell and hardly even notice it's there at all that's how much space I have for my legs and feet. The airlines could take a leaf out of their book I reckon. It's interstate and carrying a lot of long-distance passengers. I think it's going all the way to Chicago but I'm getting off at the second stop. There's another AT hiker a few seats back from me, her name is Rocky and she's also disembarking at Harpers Ferry. We go into the town together, grab a bite to eat, and then Uber to Harpers Ferry Hostel International for the night. It's a quaint little place with super friendly staff and a well-equipped kitchen. They even give us free beer!

There are a few others here this evening. Rocky makes cookies for all of us to share, and in the morning, she whips up a batch of tasty pancakes for breakfast. She's returning to the trail after several days of recuperation having accidentally stepped on a hornet's nest resulting in a trip to the ER and several days convalescing. Earlier on in her hike, she fell on some lose rocks coming down a steep mountainside and split her head open badly and that's how she got her trail name. She's also completing her triple crown, that's walking all three of America's long-distance hiking trails – the Appalachian Trail, the Pacific Crest Trail and the Continental Divide Trail. And she's doing it all after recovering from some very serious health issues. Amazing lady...and a good cook.

In the morning we make our way to the Appalachian Trail Conservancy building and I get Rocky to take a photo of me in the same spot where I stood nearly three months ago. I look, and feel, a whole lot different now than I did then. There's a large relief map of the whole AT here. I put my index fingers on my start point at Harpers Ferry and my end point in Connecticut. The space in between them is impressive. I suddenly get a real idea of exactly how much of the trail I've covered during my walk; over one fifth of its entire length. I have a conversation with the guy behind the counter about the C & O canal route. I'm absolutely convinced that when I leave the town, I need to turn left to follow the canal path in that direction and he has to say to me three times, "No, you're going right. Downstream. Rivers flow towards the sea. Washington is near the coast. Downstream." I knew that, and I have no idea why I was so convinced I was going the opposite way; I hadn't even considered the direction of the water flow. He must have thought I was a sandwich short of a picnic. Eventually the penny drops and I realise my mistake. I feel a bit of an idiot but it's made both of us chuckle. So, it turns out then, that the first three miles that I walk today are the *same* first three miles that I walked on the AT all those weeks ago. There were no leaves on the trees back then and it was very cold. It feels right somehow that I have come full circle back to the beginning.

Rocky points out some well camouflaged turtles, and once my eye gets accustomed to what I'm looking out for, I see a lot more of them. They sit on the half-submerged logs in the middle of the water, their backs covered in duck weed.

We see the rippling trail that a water moccasin has left in the green blanket that coats the water's surface. She walks with me until the trails divide and then she peels off to the left, following the AT up an incline and disappearing out of site rapidly. She's headed off to Maine and I'm on my way to Washington.

CHAPTER FOURTEEN
Fifty miles of flat

I see a blue heron hiding in the shallows behind the low hanging branches of a tree growing on the bank, and a woodpecker that keeps spiralling its way up a tree trunk, cleverly moving out of view every time I point my camera in its direction. A little later a deer crosses the path ahead of me. The terrain is easy and flat, exactly what you would expect a canal towpath to be. No surprises here. There are even encouraging little wooden marker posts at regular intervals displaying the mile number you're passing, counting down to mile zero in Georgetown, Washington. It's beginning to feel like I'm on a proper walking holiday.

There's a log off to one side of the track and I sit down on it to have a drink of water and a snack. A couple out for a stroll come over and we talk. He's a retired scout leader and he shares his knowledge of the local campsites and places that are close enough to get a hot meal. He even offers to carry my pack for a while but I know it's a lot heavier than it looks and I just couldn't let him do that, I don't want to be responsible for anyone getting a hernia or slipping a disc on my account. Still, I'm touched that he would offer, it's a kind thought and I tell him so.

I've heard that there's a washout between me and the hiker/biker campsite I'm planning to stay at tonight. I've been told that it may be passable on foot, but I'm not sure if that information is accurate. Besides that, I've seen a notice offering a free shuttle around the blockage, but not until the morning, so I'm not sure whether to try and make it or to stop at the Brunswick family campsite just this side of the obstruction. A guy on his way there pulls his car over next to me and winds the window down. He says that there's a severe weather warning for imminent thunder storms in place for this area and advises me to get to off the trail and find some shelter. Very soon after that, a family of cyclists also stop me. They're coming from the opposite direction and have peddled down to the washout; they couldn't get through so my decision is made for me really and I walk as far as the family campsite and pay the eight dollars for a pitch for the night.

The lady who books me in shares my first name so we have something to talk about straight away. They're very friendly and helpful and the campsite is well equipped with hot showers and charging facilities. I pitch my tent and then sit under a pavilion a little way off to cook my supper…and then the heavens open. Hail stones the size of marbles hammer down all around me, I can see them bouncing off the fly sheet of my tent in the distance. I'm so glad that I didn't choose to walk the extra miles today, I'm pretty sure that those hail stones are big enough to have left bruises. When it's finally over and the sky clears, the manager comes out and walks around talking to the campers, checking up on us to make sure we're all ok it was that bad. I hear later that we got off lightly in Brunswick and that one town over they were the size of golf balls! Miraculously my tent didn't leak at all. Not a bad day. I even saw my first groundhog just before the storm hit. It was wandering about on the grass near the picnic benches with its nose in the air, presumably sniffing around for dropped food.

The shuttle around the wash out leaves from Brunswick railway station at 10am in the morning so I walk a mile back the way I came. On the path ahead of me is a large bird munching its way through some roadkill. I realise that it's a turkey vulture, the same birds that I often saw circling overhead in the mountains, I think that they're a whole heap load prettier in the sky than they are close up! I cross the railway tracks and wait. A local outfitter is providing the daily transport until the path can be cleared. It's mostly cyclists that are using the service and they never know how many people might turn up so they've laid on a minibus with a trailer, but today it's only me waiting for a lift. My driver, Matt, is a former serviceman in his late twenties. He talks about the therapeutic value of the outdoor pursuits that his job allows him to participate in and he tells me about a blind veteran friend of his who kayaked the Grand Canyon. I share my story and we talk about our hopes and dreams for the future.

I love the depth of conversation that can be shared between human beings even during such brief encounters. I've found this to be the case throughout my adventure. I wonder if it's because there's so little time that people dispense with the meaningless small talk and just cut to the chase, or whether it's about the anonymity that allows us to open up to strangers about the things in our lives that we might not be comfortable disclosing to those we see day in day out?

Matt drops me off at Point of Rocks and I continue on my way. At Nolands Ferry I sit down on a bench for a snack and a lovely lady called Lois with her three young kids, two in a buggy and one on a bike, asks me where I'm hiking from. I tell her about the Appalachian Trail and how I ended up on the towpath and she tells me that her sister would dearly love to walk the AT one day. We talk for ages. She used to live around here when she was a kid and she's made the journey here today to show her own children this beautiful area where she grew up.

For a while, I follow a bloke with a trailer attached to the back of his trike. It's got a small sunshade and I can see that he's trying to take a couple of small dogs out for a ride in it. Unfortunately, one of them keeps jumping out and each time it does he patiently stops to pick up the errant animal and replaces it in the back. Eventually he gives up trying to ride and walks the trike, it doesn't stop the dog from hopping off every so often though. It's quite comical to watch. I pass them by.

Further on, as I look into the distance it appears as though the path has completely disappeared. It seems to be covered in an awful lot of greenery. As I draw closer, I realise that a tree has gone over, and it looks like it's happened very recently. There are a couple of cyclists milling around by it, trying to break off twigs and branches in order to make a pathway through that will let them pass with their bicycles. They confirm that it must have fallen only a short while ago because when they rode through here in the other direction an hour earlier the route was clear. Then I remember a really loud noise that I heard not long ago. It sounded to me like a crack of thunder, but I thought it was some kind of fire arm and I'd paid it no attention. This is America after all…it could have been someone in their backyard doing target practice for all I knew. Making my way through the debris is a bit of a mission, and it's a lot harder for the guys lifting their bikes over the fallen wood. As I turn around and look back, I can see that a massive side branch has snapped off. It's got to be at least two-foot-thick where it joined the trunk. If anyone had been standing on the path when that fell there is no doubt that they wouldn't have stood a chance. This is a busy towpath so it's amazing it didn't kill anyone.

I cross the Monocacy aqueduct with its views over the river, and I say hello to a lady fisherman. She hasn't caught anything yet today; we decide that the hot weather has probably sent the fish into the cooler waters near the banks, where the shade provided by the vegetation offers a bit of cover. There's been a huge amount of wildlife on the towpath today, including my first live racoon sighting. The fluffy little chap, who looked a whole lot healthier than the one I saw on my first day in this country, was trying to conceal himself behind a log in a muddy, dried up section of the canal and he looked like he could do with a bit of a bath. His black and white cheeky face looked so cute peeking out from his hiding place.

I stop for the night at Marble Quarry hiker/biker campsite. I can't decide where to pitch my tent. I'm very mindful of what's overhead after the fallen tree today. The only suitable spot seems to be next to another tent that's already pitched. There's a lady tending a small fire just off to one side and I assume its hers. I say hello, but she ignores me. She's seen me so I'm pretty certain it isn't because she is hard of hearing. I try again but no response so I go ahead and put my tent up anyway. She walks over and literally picks up her entire tent, which isn't pegged to the ground, and walks to the other end of the site with it. She comes back and picks up her bike and wheels that away too. Well, alright then. What's that all about? She's dressed strangely, like she has layers of rags on, one over another and she's coughing in a very unhealthy manner. I'm pretty certain that she's not a homeless person as there are regular patrols along the canal enforcing the 'one night only' rule about staying, and I notice that her equipment isn't cheap either when I see her blowing up her air mattress later. I feel unsettled and I imagine her bringing out a concealed weapon in the night and stabbing me to death or something. All this time I've been out here and it's the first time that I have a genuine moment of anxiety. I WhatsApp one of my daughters and get her to ring me, making sure my phone is turned up really loud so that Coughing Woman will definitely be able to hear it. I have a very loud conversation, ensuring that I'm quite clear about my location so she knows that someone else knows where I am…and if they need to find a body they'll know where to start dredging the river. I calm down a bit and decide I'm overreacting. Later on, I see her struggling to work the very old and stiff water pump so I decide to take my life in my hands and do the decent thing by asking her if she wants any help. She gruffly replies, "I'm doing it aren't I?" Well, that was rude! Still, I restrain myself and explain that I saw that it appeared to be hard work and I just thought that I could make it easier for her. I leave it at that. At least I know she can talk and just doesn't want to. I respect her privacy and leave her alone.

There's a lot of coughing coming from the other end of the campsite in the night, but I wake up alive in the morning, no stab wounds, no bullet holes. I can't believe I actually thought a sick, elderly woman would be a threat! In fact, I'm now beginning to feel sorry for her and I hope she gets that cough seen to real soon.

I force myself to swallow a bit of oatmeal for breakfast. I thought I would give it another try the last time I resupplied as it's so much lighter to carry than granola and, even though this terrain is infinitely better than the mountains, my feet and knees still hurt. But I'm clearly not over the whole oatmeal overkill thing yet. I persuade two litres of water out of the insanely noisy pump, which makes a metallic squealing sound loud enough to threaten to deafen me and rivals the effect that scraping your fingernails down a blackboard has on my teeth. I make my way down the path still a bit hungry.

My hunger is soon addressed though when I get to White's Ferry. There's an actual cable ferry here. It transports vehicles over the Potomac river from the Maryland side I'm on to the opposite bank in Virginia. It reminds me of the King Harry Ferry in Cornwall, England. I watch it load up and set off. It's basically an open platform that can hold maybe a dozen cars at the most. There's hardly anything else here apart from the ferry…except for a store and grill. I order a cheese burger and take it to the park just over the back and sit on a picnic bench to eat it. Oh, my goodness! Best. Burger. Ever. I don't know what they've done to produce something so succulent and tasty, even the bun is a superior quality, and I don't think that it's because I'm hungry either. I've had a fair few burgers since I've been here and not one of them has even come close to this. I'm so impressed that I even leave a review on google maps. After I dump my trash in the toilets by the park entrance, I make a second visit, this time to get a coffee. I sit in and do a bit of mobile phone charging whilst I drink it.

As I'm sitting there, a couple come in. They're debating what to choose from the menu so I tell them to have the burger because it's the best one that I have tasted since I've been in America. The gentleman, Dan, astutely says that the strength of my recommendation very much depends on exactly how long I've been in the States and exactly how many burgers I've eaten whilst I've been here. I tell them my story and we end up having a long and interesting conversation. They're from Florida and have come up to visit their grandchildren who are graduating this week. The subject turns to politics, as it so often does; when anyone finds out that I'm British they always want to know what I think about Brexit. It's interesting listening to what people think about the events taking place back home, and about how they perceive the direction that politics is taking in their own country. Linda, his wife, wants to know what the British public think of the American populous in view of the current elected leader and whether the people at home have bought into the picture of them that's often portrayed in the popular press. I reassure them that anyone whose opinion is worth anything is bright enough to know better than to swallow what the tabloid press writes. I'm really enjoying the stimulating conversation; they're intelligent and articulate and it's a pleasure spending time talking with them. Dan asks me what I've found to be the most unexpected thing on my travels. I tell him that, hands down, it's definitely been the lack of health and safety legislation on the trail. I remark that this wouldn't happen in the UK...there'd be railings or at the very least, warning signs.

He laughs and recounts the tale of a canoe trip they took one evening whilst holidaying somewhere abroad. Health and safety weren't in the local guide's vocabulary either. He said something about getting a bit too close to some crocodiles in the dark...or it might have been hippos, I can't recall which now, but the point was that he remembers thinking, "This wouldn't happen in the United States". I leave them to eat their food in peace and as we part, Dan tells me that I should take a huge amount of self-pride in what I've achieved so far. I realise he's right. It was something. It really was.

I walk slowly on. I do a lot of lollygagging (apparently this translates to "dawdling" in English) and take lots of photos today. The towpath is sandwiched in between the canal, which is mostly overgrown and unused, and the Potomac river, and there's an extraordinary amount of wildlife here. Dragonflies of every shape, size and colour fly around me, as do striking butterflies in shades of iridescent blue, stripy black and white with swallow tails, and many other variations besides. Blue herons, White egrets, and turtles inhabit the canal along the stretches that still have water. There are often deer crossing the path ahead of me, some of them quite close. I've seen snakes in the undergrowth either side of me, and on one occasion I nearly stepped on one because I was too busy daydreaming to pay attention to where I was putting my feet. On stretches where the trees are close together, giving dense coverage, I've seen a lot of black coloured Grey squirrels. Apparently, this is a melanistic variety that used to be much more common before the European settlers arrived and started to remove the forests for building and firewood. This mutation becomes more common the further north you go within the Grey squirrel's range because the woodland becomes denser and the black colouration makes it harder for overhead predators to spot them, and also because they seem to cope better with the lower temperatures than their paler counterparts. I really like this trail, it's peaceful, flat and full of nature.

Chisel Branch hiker/biker campsite is close to the river and it has a beautiful view. There's easy access down to the beach which is strewn with driftwood. I think I might try and make a fire tonight. I'm here on my own and I stroll down to the water's edge for a bit. It's strange to think that I've only got a couple more nights left sleeping in a tent and that in just over a week I'll be home. I settle down to my normal camp duties, getting water, making dinner, and tonight, collecting fire wood. When I'm done eating, I build a little pyramid from tiny twigs over a pile of wood shavings that supports a Vaseline soaked cotton wool ball carefully balanced on top of it. One spark from my all singing all dancing fire striker and it's lit. First time. I'm so pleased with myself. Who needs a gas lighter, eh? I congratulate myself, and an internal feeling of serious smugness starts to settle in. I have clearly arrived; I'm a fully-fledged expert – Bear Grylls eat your heart out. I continue to feed it ever increasingly sized pieces of wood until I have quite a respectable fire going.

Whilst I'm doing a decent impression of a pyromaniac, another hiker pulls into camp from the Washington direction. He seems to be engrossed in setting up his gear, and after last night's experience, I decide to let him sort himself out before I go over and introduce myself. In the meantime, one of the C & O canal patrol guys also turns up. These volunteers ride up and down the towpath on their bikes wearing their official high viz vests, checking that everything's ok and nothing untoward is going on. I could have done with him yesterday. He's ridden over to the new guy and they're chatting away. I go over and join the conversation. He turns out to be a fount of knowledge and takes us on a short walk back up the path to a hidden sideroad. There's what's left of an impressive lock there, concealed by the undergrowth. It's unusual in that it has a turn in it; the lock isn't straight. He tells us its history. Apparently, the people on the Virginia side of the Potomac wanted a slice of the action when cargo was being carried on the canal many years ago, so they commissioned this lock. There's a matching one on the other side of the river that is just about visible if you know where to look. In the end it was hardly used. We'd have never found it if the patrol bloke hadn't shown it to us. That's not the only thing he shares either. He's got a stash of raw carrot sticks that he hands out to us. He also mentions that there are wild mulberries in season and encourages us to look out for the fruiting trees. I ask him about the wild strawberries I've seen. They're just like the ones back home but when I tried them, they were dry and tasteless. He tells me that he's not surprised they tasted awful, technically they're inedible. Pity as I've seen loads of them, and if they'd tasted like English ones, I'd have foraged for them at every available opportunity. After a predictable conversation about politics, he carries on down the path on his bike.

My camp mate's name is Bobby. He's walking a coast to coast route, from one side of the US to the other. He's impressed by my fire lighting skills, I'm more impressed by the fact that I got it going again after it'd gone out during our guided lock trip by just blowing on it and poking it a bit. We collect more wood and keep it going until half past eleven that night. We swap stories. He's got a friend currently walking the AT, she's finding it challenging and is feeling a little disheartened. I encourage him to encourage her to keep going because I know exactly the emotional toll that the AT extracts from you, and I know the positive impact that someone rooting for you can have on your mental state too. He talks about his childhood. His father was in the American Military and he was born in Japan but spent his younger years in the UK. He grew up in Scotland and then moved to Madrid as a teenager. We share our thoughts about how the way our lives have panned out has affected who we are in terms of our plans and feelings about the future. It's an honest and deep conversation, two people both trying to find their place in the world. As we speak, all around us in the vegetation there's the backdrop of a bioluminescent lightshow put on for us by myriads of fireflies lighting up their tiny glowing bottoms and flashing them at us.

Before I leave the next day, I tell Bobby that he absolutely has to get a burger at the Grill in White's Ferry, and then I'm off on my way. I end up walking just over thirteen and a half miles today. I was going to stop at Horsepen Branch hiker/biker campsite, but after sitting down at the bench there for a snack I decided I really didn't want to have my blood sucked dry tonight. It was teeming with mozzies, and on top of that, there wasn't one safe spot that didn't have overhanging elderly looking tree branches, so I walked on, and don't my feet know it now. They really hurt. And I'm tired. It's been hot. I'm much further south than I was and the temperature here is a lot warmer, it's reaching twenty-four degrees Celsius by ten in the morning every day. The heat saps your energy and it's hard to stay hydrated.

Swains Lock hiker/biker campsite is right by the river again, and I'm treated to an awesome view for the second night running. There are designated camping spots and there's a water fountain and a bank of Portaloos. I take a walk toward the river's edge in the evening and I very nearly step on a snake hiding in the low undergrowth. It's curled itself up into a knot with its head poised over its coiled body looking straight at me with its mouth open as though it's ready to strike. I recognise its colour, pattern and behaviour to be that of a young water moccasin or cotton mouth. This semi-aquatic venomous viper is an incredibly good swimmer that tends to come ashore at night and hide in low growing vegetation. I saw a guy camped at the other end of the site bathing in the river earlier on this evening so I walk down there to warn him that they're about. He's French and he's never heard of water moccasins and he has very limited English. I have to describe the snake to him and explain why it's a seriously bad idea to be wondering around in the dark through the low blanket of weeds that covers much of the site.

I get an early night. My legs look like pin cushions. I've been bitten to death today despite the copious quantities of DEET I've been smothering myself in. I think it's all run off though; even my ankles were sweating it's been so ridiculously hot. It's a sticky night and it rains, but there's no storm to clear the air

I leave late in the morning. I've decided I've done my last night of camping in the States. There are fifteen miles left to go and this is the last tent site before mile zero in Georgetown, DC, where the trail ends. I can't walk them all in one go, besides, it's evil hot and there are storms forecast…and I stink, so I'm going as far as Seven Locks, which is about half way. I'll spend the night in a motel and finish up the last leg in the morning.

Today's highlight is Great Falls Park. Before walking to the overlook to see the falls, I pop into the visitor centre, grab a very long drink and a snack from the concession stand and sit down on a picnic bench in the shade to enjoy them. I have company in the shape of a small black and white striped lizard with an awesome blue tail. Shockingly, I also notice some warning signs written in no less than three languages, they even use the word "danger" in white lettering on a red background. Apparently, if I value my life, I should stay off the rocks at the water's edge and refrain from swimming and wading because of the extremely strong current and undertow. I look over the railing and see two clearly suicidal kayakers weaving in and out of the rocks in the white water. Maybe that's why there are so few health and safety notices around.

The falls are amazing, the force of the water flowing over the rocks at a break neck speed creates a deafening roar. I have a bird's eye view from where I'm standing and I can see that the water splits, running on either side of sizable rocky protrusions, cascading ever downwards in a violent white spewing froth. It makes me feel quite nauseous leaning over the edge of the railing watching the water descend beneath me. This is what thirty-five thousand years of erosion looks like. The river drops nearly eighty feet in under a mile.

I return to the peace of the canal towpath and pretty soon I find a bench tucked into a clearing to the side of the path where I rest for a bit and watch the water in the canal. Something moves just below the surface leaving behind it a series of ripples, expanding in ever increasing concentric circles. It makes me think that my life, and I guess everyone else's too, is just like that. The actions that we take cause ripples that flow outwards, and as we pass through time and space, their effects impact those around us, sometimes fleetingly with little consequence, and sometimes permanently, changing the course of people's lives, and we never know the impact, good or bad, that we have had.

I walk the remaining miles to Seven Locks in the blistering heat. I'm incredibly grateful for the aircon once I get to my motel room. Only one more day of hiking left.

My Uber driver in the morning is called Tsega, he's originally from Ethiopia. His father was a government official for Haile Selassie, and his family had no choice but to flee when things started to go sideways in the seventies. He clearly loves Ethiopia and enthusiastically recounts a tale of when he was a safari guide back in the day. He was taking a couple of tourists to the wild south of the country when the radiator on their truck blew out as they were fording a river. He had to leave two of the three game wardens with the couple whilst he and the other one walked out to the nearest town to get help. On their way they saw an old she-buffalo, and then a bit later they heard lions roaring in the distance from behind them. They hoped that the ones they'd left behind hadn't ended up as the cats' dinner. They eventually got to a town two days later and drove the five hours back to the broken truck with a mechanic in tow. On their drive back, they'd passed the carcass of the old she-buffalo, dead and eaten by lions. The couple they'd left behind were sure that Tsega had died the night that he left because they'd heard the roaring lions too and assumed the worst. That she-buffalo had unknowingly saved all their lives by losing her own. Great story.

I struggle to walk today, it's blisteringly hot, my feet hurt so much and my knees aren't happy. There's a sign post on the side of the river to my right, it's angled so as to be obviously visible to water traffic…they'd find it hard to miss though – it's the size of a house with foot high letters. Clearly, they have saved up all their safety warning notices and ploughed their efforts into just this one. In red letters, it reads: "STOP. DAM AHEAD. DEADLY UNDERTOW. GET TO SHORE." I guess they're hoping that even the foolhardiest kayaker will take notice of this very serious looking sign. I lose sight of the river further down, and just past a parking area where I briefly stop to purchase yet another long, cold drink, there's an old guy cleaning litter out of the canal. He gives me some tips on what to see in the city, and some strong opinions on what he thinks about the president.

The last few miles are difficult; it's not straightforward following the canal through Georgetown but eventually I find the last marker post – mile zero. I've done it! I sit down on a bench and rest my legs for a bit. I've still got to get to my hostel and it looks like I'm going to have to walk the two miles to get there as the secret police have closed off the roads out of Georgetown. How do I know it's the secret police? Because their cars have sign writing on them that says "United States Secret Service" …how is that 'secret' then?? Still, it's not all bad, my walk takes me right past the front of the White House and a large gathering of protestors, I'm told later that they are a permanent fixture.

The next three days I spend sightseeing. I visit Arlington Cemetery and watch the changing of the guard at the Tomb of the Unknown Soldier. Those guys don't miss a syllable or a step, so absolutely precise, the attention to detail is mesmerising and if I didn't know they were people I would

169

have said it was AI. Huge respect. I've seen Gibbs from NCIS on TV here so many times, it's weird to be standing in this place in real life. The Korean war memorial is eerie. Life sized sculptures of troops in their coats and helmets, each one an individual, are caught in a snapshot of time. Their shadows reflect in the shiny marble of the wall running alongside where they stand, providing a ghostly backdrop to the troops faces etched on the surface. The Vietnam War memorial has so many names, such a sad loss of life. As I walk amongst the numerous veterans and their families, it's hard not to cry and I'm glad that I'm wearing sunglasses and carrying tissues.

I spend an afternoon in the Smithsonian. There's a nice exhibit on rocks, the caption reads "All cracked up. Do you see a pattern?" I laugh, it sounds like a very accurate description of my journey on the Appalachian Trail. I'm treated to great view of the city from the Old Post Office and Clocktower, located in the Trump Hotel building, and it's free. Bonus. I visit the Library of Congress where I see the Guttenberg Bible and Thomas Jefferson's Library. The building kind of reminds me a bit of the Natural History Museum in London. At one point, I even get mistaken for a homeless person! There's a couple handing out sandwiches from the back of a white van. I've got some friends who run a charity helping the homeless people in my home town so I'm interested to talk to these guys about their experiences here in Washington. As I make my way over towards them, one of them starts to approach me, brandishing a sandwich. I have to quickly explain that I'm actually a hiker and not a vagrant. It's a good job that I'm not bothered by what people think of my appearance...I've been in a lot of public places over the last few days without a backpack, I smile when I realise what people must have been thinking. Washington is an interesting city, there's so much in one place here. I think I like it.

On my last day, I pack my gear. It's much lighter now than when I first began, there doesn't seem to be so much of it anymore. I get the tube and then a bus to the airport. I arrive with hours to spare before I have to check in for my flight and the kind lady on the desk suggests that I take a bus to the Udvar-Hazy Centre. It's a national space and aviation museum twelve minutes bus ride away and the money to build it was provided by a Hungarian, Steven F. Udvar-Hazy, in 1999. The space shuttle Discovery is housed here, as are pieces of Apollo 11. It hadn't dawned on me until now that in three weeks' time it will be the fiftieth anniversary of man's landing on the moon. When I was just a couple weeks old, I sat on my dad's lap in front of our television and watched those historic events unfold. How poignant that my adventure ends as it started on the plane journey here, with thoughts of my father.

EPILOGUE

Five hundred miles done...and home.

I caught my plane home with no dramas. The night I returned was a Wednesday and my daughter dropped me straight to my homegroup which was meeting that evening as usual. Everyone said I'd shrunk. I know I've dropped at least two dress sizes. My knees were still shot and I was having trouble bearing weight, particularly on the left one, so my people gathered round, as they do, and asked God to sort it out. The next day I was doing one legged squats with it…I guess that's probably what you'd call a miracle. I'm not surprised. God's been with me throughout the whole of my journey, He just kept turning up again and again. The other leg's getting there slowly, it's still not ok, but I'll take what I can get.

This whole experience has reinforced for me that life is a gift. Ok, sometimes life dishes out lemons; because of our own choices, because of other people's choices, or just because we live in an imperfect world full of flaws. But even if we end up with a glass half empty, we can still be grateful that we have a glass at all, and that it's not broken, and even if it is – go get some duct tape and make lemonade…and then share it. Smile at the people you pass on the street, say thank you to the checkout operator, let that guy out at the junction when you're driving, say hello to that neighbour with the noisy dog. It costs nothing, but it might be worth a fortune to them. Life is a gift.

I went on this journey because I wanted to do something extraordinary and to test my mettle. I reckon I can tick both of those boxes! I've learnt that I can do much more than I thought I could, that being brave is about being terrified and doing it anyway, that being wise is about acknowledging your limits and listening to your body. I've gained an understanding of my vulnerability and made peace with it; I know that sometimes I am afraid and sometimes I am lonely, and that's ok. And, above all, I've learnt that adventure is seventy-five percent type two fun.

And now? I guess I feel just a little displaced. I have no idea what's next…and I'm not that bothered that I don't know what's next either because I know that whatever it is, it's probably going to be alright. Would I go back? Would I try and complete the rest of the trail? Maybe…we'll see…

Thanks for reading. If you enjoyed this book, please consider leaving an honest review on Amazon

Made in the USA
Monee, IL
31 January 2023

26555213R00111